LET'S MAKE IT SIMPLE

SHUBHAM DUMBRE

"Let's Make IT Simple"

is dedicated to all pure hearts and souls on this planet!

- Shubham Dumbre -

Contents

Contents

Acknowledgements

This book is officially published by Delta The Innovators (DTI)

www.deltatheinnovators.com

"We are innovators, who regularly work hard and smart to create an alchemy of marvelous products, operational excellence and pioneering customer services by empowering talents with eternal opportunities to discover their best, right from their nascent stage.

We believe in simplifying things by gaining all sorts of challenging experiences and by coming up with quality results that will benefit the world."

DTI is a stalwart philanthropic syndicate that has firmly impacted more than 10000+ people by imparting education and by providing innovative technical solutions regularly.

Preface

About Shubham Dumbre (Founder, Delta The Innovators):

- **LinkedIn Profile:** www.linkedin.com/in/ishubhamdumbre
- **Personal Website:** www.ishubhamdumbre.home.blog
- **Instagram Profile:** www.instagram.com/ishubhamdumbre_
- **Facebook Profile:** www.facebook.com/ishubhamdumbre
- **Email ID:** ishubhamdumbre@gmail.com
- **Official Website:** www.deltatheinnovators.com
- **YouTube:** www.youtube.com/c/deltatheinnovators

• • •

First Impression 2022

• • •

Prologue

"**Let's Make IT Simple**" is one of my most ambitious projects till date. I have always loved technology, experimentation, learning, innovation, efficiency, creativity along with connectivity, and have admired their endless possibilities together.

The IT dimension is vast, constantly upgrading, and is moving ahead with an incredible pace. I came across 'n' number of instances where my thoughts began to move and shape in this direction of creating something that would benefit everyone, regardless of their experience, location, situations, understanding, exposure and bank balance. This book is a worthy answer to all those queries, dilemmas, choices, decisions, challenges, actions and outcomes that we've come across at some point or the other. It is a humble effort to simplify complexities within timeframes in an effective manner.

This volume is a library of **2500+** useful resources that can be utilised for the greater good of people globally. I've tried my best to explore and research on each of these resources individually, to select the most supreme, secure, advanced and open ones from the rest. When I had started working on this book, my idea was to cover the Free Software Movement and the Open Source Initiative, which later matured towards covering this magnanimous concept of "**Let's Make IT Simple**".

Awareness is the path and execution is the key of inventions, results and the impact that one can attain in a lifetime. Generations ahead are benefited with the breakthroughs that we can achieve today, and so I took up this critical responsibility of making everyone aware of the resources that we possess now.

Stephen Hawking had said, "We all are now connected by the Internet, like neurons in a giant brain". I resonate with this idea of connectivity, and so in order to accelerate the use of IT resources in all explored and unexplored areas of our world spectrum, I gift you all with this useful, safe, sorted, tested and verified smart resource toolkit, known as - **Let's Make IT Simple**.

The Foundation

"As we enjoy great advantages from the inventions of others, we should be glad of an opportunity to serve others by any invention of ours, and this we should do freely and generously."

- Benjamin Franklin

Our actions are driven by the situations that we face. These actions can lead to 'n' number of consequences, permutations and combinations. Sometimes, these actions result in path breaking innovations. The foundation of **"Free Software"** too, is an outcome of such a situation.

In the 1980's, at the Massachusetts Institute of Technology (MIT) laboratory, hacker Richard and his associates were allowed to change the code of printers so that they produced understandable error messages. This was convenient for the users, as the printers automatically gave the error messages in case of any issues, which would help the users to fix those efficiently. One day, a new printer arrived, which restricted these hackers from accessing its program to modify it. They tried their best to change it, but it was forbidden. The lack of understandable error messages in this case caused a lot of inconvenience for the users. As the new printer was operating on a proprietary non-free software, no one other than the software company was in a position to change its code. It was an unwanted dependency where the software company controlled and charged the printer users for any alterations. This is where Richard was convinced that software should be free and the roots of free software began to grow deeper.

Richard Matthew Stallman, popularly known by his initials **RMS**, is an American MIT hacker who started the **Free Software Movement** in the 1980's. He launched a free software operating system titled as the **GNU** project in **1983**. GNU is a recursive acronym for **GNU's Not Unix**. The free software movement is one of the most successful social movements to arise from computing culture, driven by a worldwide community of ethical programmers dedicated to the cause of freedom and sharing.

In the early computing era, AT&T Bell Laboratories had developed an operating system named **Unix**. At that point of time, the Unix operating system was a dominant proprietary non-free operating system. Stallman's GNU is similar to Unix, but it uses free software instead of the non-free Unix code.

Richard Stallman advocates "Freedom" and his idea with the GNU project was to create an operating system just like Unix, with openly available source code that could be accessed, altered, modified, copied, reengineered and redistributed. Multiple libraries, programs, packages, applications, tools and resources are released under the branches of the GNU Project.

The term "free" refers to being able to do what you want with the code, rather than the code being free of charge just in terms of price. The term "free software" is prone to misinterpretation: an unintended meaning, "software you can get for zero price," fits the term just as well as the intended meaning, "software which gives the user certain freedoms." In Stallman's explanations, we find **Free as in freedom, not as in free beer."** Laws of a community are free when they make their control knowable, and they are open to change. Free software is control that is transparent, open to change, just as free laws, rules, rights and regulations. Stallman's Free Software Movement aims to make code transparent, and subject to change, by rendering it "free."

At a technology conference, Richard explained the need for free softwares with an interesting example - "Imagine if you bought a house and the basement was locked and only the original building contractor had the key. If you needed to make any change, repair anything, you'd have to go to him, and if he was too busy doing something else he'd tell you to get lost and you'd be stuck. You are at that person's mercy and you become downtrodden and resigned. That's what happens when the blueprints to a computer program are kept secret by the organisation that sells it. That's the usual way things are done."

The program in a Unix-like system that allocates machine resources and talks to the hardware is called the **Kernel**. GNU's own kernel, the **GNU Hurd**, was started in 1990. Back then there was a better alternative to the GNU Hurd, known as **Linux**. The **Linux Kernel** was originally authored by **Linus Torvalds** in 1991 for his personal computer. It is a free and open-source, monolithic, modular, multitasking, Unix-like operating system kernel. Linux is deployed on a wide variety of computing systems, such as embedded devices, mobile devices including its use in the Android operating system, personal computers, servers, mainframes, and supercomputers.

As it met all the necessary requirements effectively back then, **GNU** adopted the **Linux Kernel**. This combination is therefore known as the **GNU/Linux** operating system. The GNU operating system is distributed under a **copyleft licence**, which uses copyright to allow users to use, modify, copy, and redistribute the software. The GNU/Linux operating system is used by millions, but is mostly referred to as "Linux" only, which is an incomplete reference. Anyone is permitted to modify and redistribute GNU, but no distributor is allowed to restrict its further redistribution. The continuous development of the GNU/Linux operating system is the critical example of the technology collaboration model. The excellent stability and security of GNU/Linux, both in server and consumer versions, is a pivotal example of success.

Stallman pioneered the concept of copyleft, which uses the principles of copyright law to preserve the right to use, modify, and distribute free software. He is the main author of free software licences which describe those terms, most notably the **GNU General Public Licence (GPL)**, the most widely used free software licence. He devised four **Freedoms 0, 1, 2 and 3** to distinguish free softwares from the rest. When a software is called "free," it means that it respects the users' essential freedoms: the freedom to run it, to study and change it, and to redistribute copies with or without changes.

According to Richard Stallman, a program is **Free Software** if the program users have the **Four Essential Freedoms**:

- **Freedom 0**: The freedom to run the program as you wish, for any purpose.
- **Freedom 1**: The freedom to study how the program works, and change it so it does your computing as you wish. Access to the source code is a precondition for this.
- **Freedom 2**: The freedom to redistribute copies so you can help your neighbour.

- **Freedom 3**: The freedom to distribute copies of your modified versions to others. By doing this you can give the whole community a chance to benefit from your changes. Access to the source code is a precondition for this.

The first two freedoms mean each user can exercise individual control over the program. With the other two freedoms, any group of users can together exercise collective control over the program. With all four freedoms, the users fully control the program. If any of them is missing or inadequate, the program is proprietary, non-free, and unjust. So, in short,

- Freedom 0 and Freedom 1 - **Individual Control**
- Freedom 2 and Freedom 3 - **Collective Control**

Free software means that the users have the freedom to run, edit, contribute to, and share the software. Thus, free software is a matter of liberty, not price. In his biography, Richard Stallman states - "My project is to make all software free. Paid software leaves people helpless and vacillating, forbidding them to share and modify it. A free operating system is the foundation for people to be able to use computers freely."

The GNU Project is part of the Free Software Movement, a campaign for freedom for users of software. It is a mistake to associate GNU with the term "**Open Source**"- that term was coined in 1998 by people who disagree with the Free Software Movement's ethical values. They use it to promote an amoral approach to the same field. The **Open Source Initiative** was led by **Bruce Perens** and **Eric S. Raymond** from 1998. Free software is a political movement while open source is a development model.

"**Open Source Initiative**" definition - Open source doesn't just mean access to the source code. The distribution terms of open-source software must comply with the following criteria:

- **Free Redistribution** - The licence shall not restrict any party from selling or giving away the software as a component of an aggregate software distribution containing programs from several different sources. The licence shall not require a royalty or other fee for such sale.
- **Source Code** - The program must include source code, and must allow

distribution in source code as well as compiled form. Where some form of a product is not distributed with source code, there must be a well-publicised means of obtaining the source code for no more than a reasonable reproduction cost, preferably downloading via the Internet without charge. The source code must be the preferred form in which a programmer would modify the program. Deliberately obfuscated source code is not allowed. Intermediate forms such as the output of a preprocessor or translator are not allowed.

- **Derived Works** - The licence must allow modifications and derived works, and must allow them to be distributed under the same terms as the licence of the original software.
- **Integrity of the Author's Source Code** - The licence may restrict source-code from being distributed in modified form only if the licence allows the distribution of "patch files" with the source code for the purpose of modifying the program at build time. The licence must explicitly permit distribution of software built from modified source code. The licence may require derived works to carry a different name or version number from the original software.
- **No Discrimination Against Persons or Groups** - The licence must not discriminate against any person or group of persons.
- **No Discrimination Against Fields of Endeavor** - The licence must not restrict anyone from making use of the program in a specific field of endeavour. For example, it may not restrict the program from being used in a business, or from being used for genetic research.
- **Distribution of Licence** - The rights attached to the program must apply to all to whom the program is redistributed without the need for execution of an additional licence by those parties.
- **Licence Must Not Be Specific to a Product** - The rights attached to the program must not depend on the program's being part of a particular software distribution. If the program is extracted from that distribution and used or distributed within the terms of the program's licence, all parties to whom the program is redistributed should have the same rights as those that are granted in conjunction with the original software distribution.
- **Licence Must Not Restrict Other Software** - The licence must not place restrictions on other software that is distributed along with the licensed software. For example, the licence must not insist that all other programs distributed on the same medium must be open-source software.

- **Licence Must Be Technology Neutral** - No provision of the licence may be predicated on any individual technology or style of interface.

Open Source licences are licences that comply with the Open Source Definition - in brief, they allow software to be freely used, modified, and shared.

The terms "**free software**" and "**open source**" stand for almost the same range of programs. However, they say deeply **different** things about those programs, based on different **values**. The free software movement campaigns for freedom for the users of computing; it is a movement for freedom and justice. This is a matter of freedom, not price, so think of "free speech," not "free beer." By contrast, the open source idea values mainly practical advantage and does not campaign for principles. As per FSF, Open Source pays no attention to right and wrong, it only is focused on popularity and success. This is why free software activists do not agree with open source, and do not use that term.

According to FSF, a software can be said to serve its users only if it respects their freedom. Malicious features, such as spying on the users, restricting the users, back doors, and imposed upgrades are common in proprietary software. Under pressure from the movie and record companies, software for individuals to use is increasingly designed specifically to restrict them. This malicious feature is known as **Digital Restrictions Management (DRM)**. This simply means controlling the users, restricting their freedom.

Open source stands for criteria a little looser than those of free software. Some open source licences are too restrictive, so they do not qualify as free licences. The criteria for open source are concerned solely with the licensing of the source code. The Open Source Initiative chose the term "Open Source," in founding member Michael Tiemann's words, to "dump the moralising and confrontational attitude that had been associated with free software and instead promote open source ideas on pragmatic, business-case grounds."

Open Source is an evolved **culture**, a new way to fix problems, a **modern** perspective, collaboration not isolation as **collaboration multiplies knowledge**. The impact of open source is exponential, as sharing enhances it all the time!

Richard Stallman, who is often considered as the "Father of Open Source", rejects this title himself because it does not call to mind what he sees as the value of the software - **Freedom**. He has described his **Free Software Foundation** and the **Open Source Initiative** as **separate camps** within the **same broad free-software community** and acknowledged that despite philosophical differences, proponents of open source and free software **"often work together on practical projects."**

The terms "**FLOSS**" and "**FOSS**" are used to be **neutral** between free software and open source. If neutrality is your goal, "FLOSS" is the better of the two, since it really is neutral. But if you want to stand up for freedom, using a neutral term isn't the way. Standing up for freedom entails showing people your support for freedom, i.e. the Free Software way.

- **Free Software Foundation** - https://www.fsf.org
- **Open Source Initiative** - https://opensource.org

CHAPTER I

Operating Systems

1. GNU/Linux - https://www.getgnulinux.org
2. Ubuntu - https://ubuntu.com
3. Debian - https://www.debian.org
4. Fedora - https://getfedora.org
5. Kali Linux - https://www.kali.org
6. Parrot OS - https://parrotlinux.org
7. Cent OS - https://www.centos.org
8. Chromium - https://www.chromium.org/chromium-os
9. Pure OS - https://www.pureos.net
10. Plasma OS - https://kde.org/plasma-desktop
11. Xubuntu - https://xubuntu.org
12. Microsoft Windows - https://microsoft.com/windows
13. Mac OS - https://www.apple.com/macos
14. iOS - https://www.apple.com/ios
15. iPadOS - https://www.apple.com/ipados
16. WatchOS - https://www.apple.com/watchos
17. Android - https://www.android.com
18. Ubuntu Touch - https://ubuntu-touch.io
19. React OS - https://reactos.org
20. FreeBSD - https://www.freebsd.org
21. Solus - https://getsol.us
22. Deepin - https://www.deepin.org
23. Sailfish OS - https://sailfishos.org
24. Tizen OS - https://www.tizen.org
25. Lineage OS - https://lineageos.org
26. Kai OS - https://www.kaiostech.com
27. Funtouch OS - https://www.vivoglobal.ph/funtouch
28. Graphene OS - https://grapheneos.org
29. Postmarket OS - https://postmarketos.org
30. Color OS - https://www.coloros.com
31. Miui - https://global.miui.com
32. Oxygen OS - https://www.oneplus.in/oxygenos

33. Plasma Mobile OS - https://plasma-mobile.org
34. Chrome OS - https://www.google.com/chromebook/chrome-os
35. Manjaro - https://manjaro.org
36. SteamOS - https://store.steampowered.com/steamos
37. Fuchsia - https://fuchsia.dev
38. Harmony OS - https://consumer.huawei.com/en/harmonyos
39. Whonix - https://www.whonix.org
40. Copperhead OS - https://copperhead.co
41. OpenSUSE - https://www.opensuse.org
42. Garuda Linux - https://garudalinux.org
43. Arch OS - https://archlinux.org
44. Mint OS - https://linuxmint.com
45. RedHat OS - https://www.redhat.com
46. Neptune OS - https://neptuneos.com
47. BunsenLabs - https://www.bunsenlabs.org
48. Zorin OS - https://zorin.com/os
49. Kubuntu - https://kubuntu.org
50. Linux - https://www.linux.org
51. Web OS - https://www.lg.com/global/business/webos
52. Haiku OS - https://www.haiku-os.org
53. Arca OS - https://www.arcanoae.com/arcaos
54. Wayne OS - https://wayne-os.com
55. SkyOS - https://www.skyenterprisesau.com/skyos
56. Oracle Solaris - https://www.oracle.com/solaris
57. Discreete Linux - https://www.privacy-cd.org
58. Subgraph OS - https://subgraph.com/sgos
59. Qubes OS - https://www.qubes-os.org
60. RISC OS - https://www.riscosopen.org
61. Archive OS - https://archiveos.org
62. Elementary OS - https://elementary.io
63. Parrotsec - https://www.parrotsec.org

CHAPTER II

Web Browsers

1. Google Chrome - https://www.google.com/chrome
2. Mozilla Firefox - https://www.mozilla.org/en-US/firefox/new
3. Microsoft Edge - https://www.microsoft.com/en-us/edge
4. Apple Safari - https://www.apple.com/safari
5. Brave - https://brave.com
6. Tor - https://www.torproject.org
7. Vivaldi - https://vivaldi.com
8. Opera - https://www.opera.com
9. Aloha - https://alohabrowser.com
10. DuckDuckGo - https://duckduckgo.com/app
11. Ant Browser - https://antbrowser.pro
12. Avast - https://www.avast.com/secure-browser
13. Blisk - https://blisk.io
14. Maxthon - https://www.maxthon.com
15. Palemoon - https://www.palemoon.org
16. Polarity - https://polaritybrowser.netlify.app
17. Srware - https://www.srware.net
18. Torch - https://torchbrowser.com
19. Waterfox - https://www.waterfox.net
20. Yandex Browser - https://browser.yandex.com
21. Konqueror - https://apps.kde.org/konqueror
22. ZAC Browser - https://zacbrowser.com
23. Gnome Web - https://wiki.gnome.org/Apps/Web
24. Iridium - https://iridiumbrowser.de
25. SeaMonkey - https://www.seamonkey-project.org
26. Ghost Browser - https://ghostbrowser.com
27. Dolphin Browser - https://dolphin.com
28. Icedragon - https://icedragon.comodo.com
29. Chromium - https://www.chromium.org
30. Internet Explorer - https://microsoft.com/ie
31. UC Browser - http://www.ucweb.com
32. Slimbrowser - https://www.slimbrowser.net

33. Coc Coc Browser - https://coccoc.com
34. Min Browser - https://minbrowser.org
35. Tenta - https://tenta.com
36. Onion Browser - https://onionbrowser.com
37. Midori - https://astian.org/en/midori-browser
38. Falkon - https://www.falkon.org
39. Lunascape - https://www.lunascape.org
40. UR Browser - https://www.ur-browser.com
41. Station Browser - https://getstation.com

CHAPTER III

Search Engines

1. Google Search - https://www.google.com
2. DuckDuckGo - https://duckduckgo.com
3. Bing - https://www.bing.com
4. Startpage - https://www.startpage.com
5. Search Encrypt - https://www.searchencrypt.com
6. Searx - https://searx.thegpm.org
7. Aol - https://search.aol.com
8. Ask - https://www.ask.com
9. Entireweb - https://www.entireweb.com
10. Private - https://private.sh
11. Gigablast - https://gigablast.com
12. Yandex - https://yandex.com
13. Infospace - https://www.infospace.com
14. Baidu - https://www.baidu.com
15. Lycos - https://www.lycos.com
16. Naver - https://www.naver.com
17. Wolfram Alpha - https://www.wolframalpha.com
18. Yahoo - https://www.yahoo.com
19. Seznam - https://www.seznam.cz
20. Qwant - https://www.qwant.com
21. Internet Archive - https://archive.org
22. Excite - https://www.excite.com
23. Ecosia - https://www.ecosia.org
24. Web Crawler - https://www.webcrawler.com
25. Qmamu - https://qmamu.com
26. Swisscows - https://swisscows.com
27. Dogpile - https://www.dogpile.com
28. Boardreader - https://boardreader.com
29. Egerin - https://www.egerin.com
30. Mojeek - https://www.mojeek.com
31. GMX - https://suche.gmx.net
32. Search - https://www.search.com

33. You - https://you.com
34. Oscobo - https://www.oscobo.com
35. Infinity Search - https://infinitysearch.co
36. Yep - https://yep.com
37. Metager - https://metager.org
38. Brave Search - https://search.brave.com
39. Petal Search - https://petalsearch.com
40. Susper - https://susper.com
41. IPFS Search - https://ipfs-search.com
42. Presearch - https://presearch.com
43. YaCy Search - https://yacy.net

CHAPTER IV

Office Suites

1. Microsoft Office Suite - https://www.office.com
2. Microsoft 365 - https://www.microsoft.com/en-us/microsoft-365
3. Libre Office - https://www.libreoffice.org
4. Google Workspace - https://workspace.google.com
5. Apple iWork - https://www.apple.com/iwork
6. Arcane Office - https://arcaneoffice.com
7. Free Office - https://www.freeoffice.com
8. OmniWeb - https://www.omnigroup.com
9. Apache Open Office - https://www.openoffice.org
10. Only Office - https://www.onlyoffice.com
11. SoftMaker Office - https://www.softmaker.com
12. WPS Office - https://www.wps.com
13. Zoho Office - https://www.zoho.com/office
14. OfficeSuite - https://www.officesuite.com
15. Corel WordPerfect Office - https://www.wordperfect.com
16. Calligra - https://calligra.org
17. Neo Office - https://www.neooffice.org
18. Hancom Office - https://office.hancom.com
19. Conceptdraw Office - https://www.conceptdraw.com
20. Collabora office - https://www.collaboraoffice.com
21. Polaris Office - https://www.polarisoffice.com
22. Ashampoo Office - https://www.ashampoo.com/en-us/office-free
23. Ssuite Office - https://www.ssuiteoffice.com
24. Nevron Office - https://www.nevronoffice.com

Virtual Private Networks

1. OpenVPN - https://openvpn.net
2. Proton VPN - https://protonvpn.com
3. Express VPN - https://www.expressvpn.com
4. Private Internet Access VPN - https://www.privateinternetaccess.com
5. TunnelBear - https://www.tunnelbear.com
6. NordVPN - https://nordvpn.com
7. Surf Shark - https://surfshark.com
8. IVPN - https://www.ivpn.net
9. IPVanish VPN - https://www.ipvanish.com
10. Hola - https://hola.org
11. Pritunl - https://pritunl.com
12. Mozilla VPN - https://www.mozilla.org/en-US/products/vpn
13. Mullvad VPN - https://mullvad.net
14. FreeLAN - https://freelan.org
15. Libreswan - https://libreswan.org
16. Zenmate - https://zenmate.com
17. SoftEther VPN - https://www.softether.org
18. Strongswan - https://www.strongswan.org
19. Tinc - https://www.tinc-vpn.org
20. WireGuard - https://www.wireguard.com
21. Shadowsocks - https://shadowsocks.org
22. Avast Secureline VPN - https://www.avast.com/secureline-vpn
23. LogMeIn Hamachi - https://www.vpn.net
24. HMA VPN - https://www.hidemyass.com
25. Pure VPN - https://www.purevpn.com
26. Windscribe - https://windscribe.com
27. Safer VPN - https://www.safervpn.com
28. CyberGhost VPN - https://www.cyberghostvpn.com
29. TorGuard VPN - https://torguard.net
30. VPN Unlimited - https://www.vpnunlimited.com
31. Hotspot Shield - https://www.hotspotshield.com
32. Urban VPN - https://www.urban-vpn.com

33. Hide - https://hide.me
34. Privado VPN - https://privadovpn.com
35. Atlas VPN - https://atlasvpn.com
36. Turbo VPN - https://turbovpn.com
37. ClearVPN - https://clearvpn.com
38. VPNBook - https://www.vpnbook.com
39. Vyprvpn - https://www.vyprvpn.com
40. Norton VPN - https://us.norton.com/products/norton-secure-vpn
41. Hoxx VPN - https://hoxx.com

CHAPTER VI

Email + Webmail

1. Google Gmail - https://workspace.google.com/products/gmail
2. Microsoft Outlook - https://outlook.com
3. Apple iCloud Mail - https://www.icloud.com/mail
4. Proton Mail - https://proton.me/mail
5. Yandex Mail - https://mail.yandex.com
6. Yahoo Mail - https://mail.yahoo.com
7. Zoho Mail - https://www.zoho.com/mail
8. Tutanota - https://tutanota.com
9. Mozilla Thunderbird - https://www.thunderbird.net
10. AOL Mail - https://mail.aol.com
11. Mailbird - https://www.getmailbird.com
12. Postbox - https://www.postbox-inc.com
13. eM Client - https://www.emclient.com
14. Airmail - https://airmailapp.com
15. INKY Mail - https://www.inky.com
16. Hiri Mail - https://www.hiri.com
17. Spike - https://www.spikenow.com
18. Edison Mail - https://www.edisonmail.com
19. Superhuman - https://superhuman.com
20. Front - https://front.com
21. Sparkmail - https://sparkmailapp.com
22. Bluemail - https://bluemail.me
23. Canarymail - https://canarymail.io
24. GMX Mail - https://www.gmx.com
25. Hushmail - https://www.hushmail.com
26. Mail - https://www.mail.com
27. Fastmail - https://www.fastmail.com
28. Mailfence - https://mailfence.com
29. Mailbox - https://mailbox.org
30. Posteo mail - https://posteo.de
31. Runbox - https://runbox.com
32. CounterMail - https://countermail.com

33. Kolab Now - https://kolabnow.com
34. Startmail - https://www.startmail.com
35. Rainloop Webmail - https://www.rainloop.net
36. Roundcube Webmail - https://roundcube.net
37. Zimbra Webmail - https://mail.zimbra.com
38. NextCloud Webmail - https://apps.nextcloud.com/apps/mail
39. Mailspring - https://getmailspring.com
40. Cypht - https://cypht.org
41. Mailpile - https://www.mailpile.is
42. SquirrelMail - https://squirrelmail.org
43. Afterlogic Webmail - https://afterlogic.org/webmail-lite
44. Litmus Webmail - https://www.litmus.com
45. Msgsafe - https://www.msgsafe.io

CHAPTER VII

Archive Programs

Archival, Extraction, ISO, etc.

1. 7 Zip - https://www.7-zip.org
2. WinZip - https://www.winzip.com
3. WinRAR - https://www.rarlab.com
4. PeaZip - https://peazip.github.io
5. The Unarchiver - https://theunarchiver.com
6. Freearc - https://www.freearc.org
7. Ark - https://apps.kde.org/ark
8. Zipware - https://www.zipware.org
9. Ashampoo Zip - https://www.ashampoo.com/en-us/zip-free
10. Hamster Zip - https://ziparchiver.hamstersoft.com
11. Bandizip - https://en.bandisoft.com/bandizip
12. IZArc - https://www.izarc.org
13. ZipGenius - https://zipgenius.com
14. Express Zip - https://www.nchsoftware.com/zip
15. Bitser - https://www.bitser.org
16. CAM UnZip - https://www.camunzip.com
17. XArchiver - https://github.com/ib/xarchiver
18. Extract - https://extract.me
19. Unzip Online - https://unzip.online
20. Createzip - https://createzip.com
21. Adobe Acrobat - https://www.adobe.com/acrobat.html
22. NX Power Lite Desktop - https://neuxpower.com/nxpowerlite-desktop
23. Powerarchiver - https://www.powerarchiver.com
24. Keka - https://www.keka.io
25. Macitbetter - https://macitbetter.com
26. ExtractNow - https://extractnow.com
27. Unarchiver One - https://cleanerone.trendmicro.com/unarchiver-one
28. Ezyzip - https://www.ezyzip.com
29. Winarchiver - https://www.winarchiver.com
30. ZIP Extractor - https://zipextractor.app
31. Rufus - https://rufuswin.com

32. PowerISO - https://www.poweriso.com
33. Imgburn - https://www.imgburn.com/
34. DoISO - https://www.ebswift.com/doiso.html
35. FreeDMG - https://www.kelleycomputing.net/freedmg

CHAPTER VIII

Digital Workspace Communication

Web Conferencing, Recording, Data Sharing, Live Streaming, Remote Screen Control, Calendar Scheduling and Community Chat, etc.

1. Zoom - https://zoom.us
2. Google Meet - https://meet.google.com
3. Microsoft Teams - https://teams.com
4. Cisco WebEx - https://www.webex.com
5. Jitsi Meet - https://meet.jit.si
6. Skype - https://www.skype.com
7. BigBlueButton - https://bigbluebutton.org
8. Fuze - https://www.8x8.com/fuze
9. Anymeeting - https://www.intermedia.com
10. HCL Sametime - https://www.hcltechsw.com/sametime
11. Jami - https://jami.net
12. Airmeet - https://www.airmeet.com
13. BlueJeans - https://www.bluejeans.com
14. Google Duo - https://duo.google.com
15. Jio Meet - https://jiomeetpro.jio.com
16. Lifesize Meeting - https://www.lifesize.com
17. Dialpad - https://www.dialpad.com
18. Mikogo - https://www.mikogo.com
19. OpenMeetings - https://openmeetings.apache.org
20. ClickMeeting - https://clickmeeting.com
21. Teamviewer - https://www.teamviewer.com
22. Alfaview - https://alfaview.com
23. Trueconf - https://trueconf.com
24. Zoho Meeting - https://www.zoho.com/meeting
25. Anydesk - https://anydesk.com
26. Devolutions - https://devolutions.net
27. Splashtop - https://www.splashtop.com
28. Airdroid - https://www.airdroid.com
29. Zoho Assist - https://www.zoho.com/assist
30. Facetime - https://www.apple.com/ios/facetime

31. Slack - https://slack.com
32. Toasty - https://toasty.ai
33. Talky - https://talky.io
34. Whereby - https://whereby.com
35. Blackboard Collaborate - https://www.blackboard.com
36. Telegram - https://telegram.org
37. WhatsApp - https://www.whatsapp.com
38. Line - https://line.me
39. Snapchat - https://www.snapchat.com
40. WeChat - https://www.wechat.com
41. Viber - https://www.viber.com
42. Voxer - https://www.voxer.com
43. Signal - https://signal.org
44. Rocket Chat - https://rocket.chat
45. Zulip - https://zulip.com
46. Paper Cups - https://papercups.io
47. Tawk - https://www.tawk.to
48. Chatwoot - https://www.chatwoot.com
49. Tinode - https://tinode.co
50. Matrix - https://matrix.org
51. Rallly - https://rallly.co
52. Flock - https://www.flock.com
53. Linphone - https://www.linphone.org
54. Wire - https://wire.com
55. Delta Chat - https://delta.chat
56. Quickblox - https://quickblox.com
57. Adamant - https://adamant.im
58. Element - https://element.io
59. Drift - https://www.drift.com
60. Intercom - https://www.intercom.com
61. Zendesk - https://www.zendesk.com
62. Digitalsamba - https://www.digitalsamba.com
63. Screenleap - https://www.screenleap.com
64. Facebook Messenger - https://www.messenger.com
65. GoToMeeting - https://www.goto.com/meeting
66. Loom - https://www.loom.com
67. Instagram Live - https://creators.instagram.com/live
68. Amazon Chime - https://app.chime.aws/meetings

69. Chrome Remote Desktop - https://remotedesktop.google.com
70. Parallels Access - https://www.parallels.com/uk/products/access
71. Adobe Connect Platform - https://www.adobe.com/products/adobeconnect.html
72. Streamyard - https://streamyard.com
73. Telestream - https://www.telestream.net/wirecast
74. Restream - https://restream.io
75. YouTube Live - https://www.youtube.com/live
76. Vimeo Livestream - https://vimeo.com/features/livestreaming
77. Brightcove - https://www.brightcove.com
78. Open Broadcaster Software - https://obsproject.com
79. Be Live - https://be.live
80. Discord - https://discord.com
81. TeamSpeak - https://teamspeak.com
82. Chanty - https://www.chanty.com
83. Tox - https://tox.chat
84. Mattermost - https://mattermost.com
85. Revolt - https://revolt.chat
86. Wickr - https://wickr.com
87. Airsend - https://www.airsend.io
88. Kosmi - https://kosmi.io
89. Gitter - https://gitter.im
90. Fosscord - https://fosscord.com
91. Nertivia - https://nertivia.net
92. Whaller - https://whaller.com
93. Daily - https://www.daily.co
94. Lark - https://www.larksuite.com
95. MiroTalk - https://p2p.mirotalk.com
96. Consolto - https://www.consolto.com
97. Yandex Telemost - https://telemost.yandex.ru
98. Spatial Chat - https://www.spatial.chat
99. SimplyVideo - https://simplyvideo.io
100. Goremote - https://goremote.fr
101. 3veta - https://3veta.com
102. Joinly - https://joinly.com
103. Pumble - https://pumble.com
104. Virola - https://virola.io
105. Tipicalls - https://tipicalls.com

106. Ring4 - https://www.ring4.com/video-meeting
107. Remote Meeting - https://www.remotemeeting.com
108. Whoosh Call - https://whooshcall.com
109. RemoteHQ - https://www.remotehq.com
110. Guilded - https://www.guilded.gg
111. Troop Messenger - https://www.troopmessenger.com
112. Lightstream - https://golightstream.com
113. Onestream - https://www.onestream.live
114. vMix - https://www.vmix.com
115. Xsplit - https://www.xsplit.com
116. Kaltura - https://corp.kaltura.com
117. Twitch - https://www.twitch.tv/p/en/stream
118. StreamShark - https://streamshark.io
119. Ecamm Live - https://www.ecamm.com/mac/ecammlive
120. Wowza - https://www.wowza.com
121. Uscreen - https://www.uscreen.tv
122. Melonapp - https://melonapp.com
123. Riverside - https://riverside.fm
124. Streamlabs - https://streamlabs.com
125. Crowdcast - https://www.crowdcast.io
126. Gather Town - https://www.gather.town
127. RingCentral - https://www.ringcentral.com
128. Book & Meet - https://bookmeet.us
129. BusyCal - https://www.busymac.com/busycal
130. Doodle - https://doodle.com
131. Calendly - https://calendly.com
132. Outlook Calendar - https://outlook.live.com/calendar
133. My Study Life - https://www.mystudylife.com
134. iCloud Calendar - https://www.icloud.com/calendar
135. Google Calendar - https://calendar.google.com
136. Boomerang - https://www.boomerangapp.com
137. CalenderHero - https://calendarhero.com
138. Tweek Calendar - https://tweek.so
139. Teamup - https://www.teamup.com
140. Fruux - https://fruux.com
141. Flexibits - https://flexibits.com/fantastical
142. Cal - https://cal.com
143. SavvyCal - https://savvycal.com

144. Discourse - https://www.discourse.org
145. Faceflow - https://www.faceflow.com
146. Fleep - https://fleep.io
147. NotePlan - https://noteplan.co
148. Yammer - https://www.yammer.com
149. Veeting - https://www.veeting.com
150. Vanilla - https://vanillaforums.com
151. Tixeo - https://www.tixeo.com
152. Startmeeting - https://www.startmeeting.com
153. Readytalk - https://www.readytalk.com
154. Meetingone - https://www.meetingone.com
155. Lucid Meetings - https://www.lucidmeetings.com
156. Live Conference Pro - https://liveconferencepro.com
157. Jostle - https://jostle.me
158. ICQ - https://icq.com
159. Free Conference Call - https://www.freeconferencecall.com
160. Bitrix24 - https://www.bitrix24.in
161. ON24 - https://www.on24.com
162. Intrado - https://www.intrado.com
163. Pexip - https://www.pexip.com
164. Smith - https://smith.ai
165. Live Webinar - https://www.livewebinar.com
166. Podium - https://www.podium.com
167. Around - https://www.around.co
168. Screen Rec - https://screenrec.com
169. Scre - https://scre.io
170. Bandicam - https://www.bandicam.com
171. Atomisystems - https://atomisystems.com
172. Techsmith - https://www.techsmith.com
173. Litecam - https://www.litecam.net
174. OBS Project - https://obsproject.com
175. Airsquirrels - https://www.airsquirrels.com
176. Telestream - https://www.telestream.net
177. Wisdom Soft - https://www.wisdom-soft.com
178. X Mirage - https://www.x-mirage.com
179. Screenpresso - https://www.screenpresso.com
180. Kapwing - https://www.kapwing.com

CHAPTER IX

Project + Team Management

CRM, ERP, Accounting, Productivity Boosters, Time Trackers, Idea Creators, Whiteboard, Collaboration Tools, Mind Mapping, Work Organiser, Analytics, Bulk Marketing Campaigns, Sales Automation, VoIP, etc.

1. Google Jamboard - https://jamboard.google.com
2. Miro - https://miro.com
3. Asana - https://asana.com
4. Clickup - https://clickup.com
5. Conceptboard - https://conceptboard.com
6. Mural - https://www.mural.co
7. ProofHub - https://www.proofhub.com
8. Nozbe - https://nozbe.com
9. Nuclino - https://www.nuclino.com
10. Explain Everything - https://explaineverything.com
11. Lucidspark - https://lucidspark.com
12. Limnu - https://limnu.com
13. Ziteboard - https://ziteboard.com
14. Fibery - https://fibery.io
15. GitMind - https://gitmind.com
16. Monday - https://monday.com
17. Lumoflow - https://lumoflow.com
18. Nutcache - https://www.nutcache.com
19. Meistertask - https://www.meistertask.com
20. Prezi - https://prezi.com
21. Canva - https://www.canva.com
22. Excalidraw - https://excalidraw.com
23. Kanban Tool - https://kanbantool.com
24. Huddle - https://huddle.com
25. Kerika - https://kerika.com
26. Loomio - https://www.loomio.org
27. Draw - https://app.diagrams.net
28. WebBoard - https://www.web-whiteboard.io

29. Stormboard - https://stormboard.com
30. Mindmup - https://www.mindmup.com
31. MindGenius - https://www.mindgenius.com
32. MindManager - https://www.mindmanager.com
33. Mindmap Ninja - https://mindmapninja.com
34. Infolio - https://www.infolio.co
35. Invision - https://www.invisionapp.com
36. Mind42 - https://mind42.com
37. Brain - https://brainio.com
38. OpenBoard - https://openboard.ch
39. Notion - https://www.notion.so
40. Trello - https://trello.com
41. 2Do - https://www.2doapp.com
42. Feng Office - https://fengoffice.com
43. Amna - https://www.getamna.com
44. Toodledo - https://www.toodledo.com
45. Todoist - https://todoist.com
46. Quire - https://quire.io
47. Coogle - https://coggle.it
48. TickTick - https://ticktick.com
49. Debategraph - https://debategraph.org
50. iMindq - https://www.imindq.com
51. MapsOfMind - https://www.mapsofmind.com
52. MindNode - https://www.mindnode.com
53. Mindomo - https://www.mindomo.com
54. Popplet - https://www.popplet.com
55. Literature & Latte - https://www.literatureandlatte.com
56. Simplemind - https://simplemind.eu
57. Restya - https://restya.com
58. Spiderscribe - https://www.spiderscribe.net
59. Twiddla - https://www.twiddla.com
60. Stemic - https://stemic.app
61. Text2Mindmap - https://tobloef.com/text2mindmap
62. Scoro - https://www.scoro.com
63. The Brain - https://www.thebrain.com
64. Elegantt - https://elegantt.com
65. Firesub - https://firesub.com
66. Getflow - https://www.getflow.com

67. WiseMapping - https://www.wisemapping.com
68. Writemapper - https://writemapper.com
69. VUE - https://vue.tufts.edu
70. nTask - https://www.ntaskmanager.com
71. Confluence - https://www.atlassian.com/software/confluence
72. Flask - https://flask.io
73. LoopedIn - https://www.loopedin.io
74. Carrot - https://carrot.io
75. DekkoSecure - https://www.dekkosecure.com
76. Frame - https://frame.io
77. Hitask - https://hitask.com
78. Freedcamp - https://freedcamp.com
79. Hightail - https://www.hightail.com
80. Float - https://www.float.com
81. Bluescape - https://www.bluescape.com
82. Flowdock - https://www.flowdock.com
83. Excelway - https://www.excelway.co
84. GroupMap - https://www.groupmap.com
85. Gqueues - https://www.gqueues.com
86. EGroupware - https://www.egroupware.org
87. Craft - https://craft.io
88. Ideaflip - https://ideaflip.com
89. Klaxoon - https://klaxoon.com
90. Lucid - https://lucid.co
91. Cardsmith - https://cardsmith.co
92. Rolljak - https://www.rolljak.com
93. Bitrix24 - https://www.bitrix24.in
94. Slatebox - https://slatebox.com
95. Whimsical - https://whimsical.com
96. Wrieda - https://wridea.com
97. Conceptdraw - https://www.conceptdraw.com
98. CardBoard - https://cardboardit.com
99. Redbooth - https://redbooth.com
100. Pivotal Tracker - https://www.pivotaltracker.com
101. Plan - https://plan.io
102. Citrix Podio - https://podio.com
103. Project Manager - https://www.projectmanager.com
104. Planview - https://www.planview.com

105. Quip - https://quip.com
106. Taiga - https://taiga.io
107. Stackfield - https://www.stackfield.com
108. Allo - https://allo.io
109. Solverboard - https://www.solverboard.com
110. Mindmeister - https://www.mindmeister.com
111. Jira - https://www.atlassian.com/software/jira
112. Accept Mission - https://www.acceptmission.com
113. 5PM - https://www.5pmweb.com
114. Omnigroup - https://www.omnigroup.com
115. Taskede - https://www.taskade.com
116. Pie - https://www.pie.me
117. Slite - https://slite.com
118. We Team - https://we.team/
119. Active Collab - https://activecollab.com
120. Teamwork - https://www.teamwork.com
121. Team Allocator - https://www.teamallocator.com
122. Advanseez - https://www.advanseez.com
123. Any - https://www.any.do
124. TeamGantt - https://www.teamgantt.com
125. Basecamp - https://basecamp.com
126. Aha - https://www.aha.io
127. Smartsheet - https://www.smartsheet.com
128. Airtable - https://www.airtable.com
129. Leadsquared - https://www.leadsquared.com
130. Seamless - https://www.seamless.ai
131. Binfire - https://www.binfire.com
132. Box - https://www.box.com
133. Breeze - https://www.breeze.pm
134. Zoho - https://www.zoho.com
135. Ayoa - https://www.ayoa.com
136. Canny - https://canny.io
137. TransparentBusiness - https://transparentbusiness.com
138. Brightidea - https://www.brightidea.com
139. Wrike - https://www.wrike.com
140. Weekdone - https://weekdone.com
141. Focus Booster - https://www.focusboosterapp.com
142. YouTrack - https://www.jetbrains.com/youtrack

143. Cacoo - https://cacoo.com
144. Ideanote - https://ideanote.io
145. Tuzzit - https://www.tuzzit.com
146. Productboard - https://www.productboard.com
147. OnceHub - https://www.oncehub.com
148. Cozi - https://www.cozi.com
149. eXo Platform - https://www.exoplatform.com
150. Xmind - https://www.xmind.net
151. Bubbl - https://bubbl.us
152. LiquidPlanner - https://www.liquidplanner.com
153. Zenkit - https://zenkit.com
154. Buildtools - https://www.ecisolutions.com/products/buildtools
155. Workzone - https://www.workzone.com
156. Chorus - https://www.chorus.ai
157. Salseken - https://www.salesken.ai
158. Salesloft - https://salesloft.com
159. Mindtickle - https://www.mindtickle.com
160. Call Tracking Metrics - https://www.calltrackingmetrics.com
161. Exotel - https://exotel.com
162. Mindtickle - https://www.mindtickle.com
163. CallRail - https://www.callrail.com
164. Twilio Flex - https://www.twilio.com
165. Toky - https://toky.co
166. Knowlarity - https://www.knowlarity.com
167. Zipteams - https://zipteams.com
168. Outreach - https://www.outreach.io
169. Convin - https://convin.ai
170. Wingman - https://www.trywingman.com
171. Salesloft - https://salesloft.com
172. OpenProject - https://www.openproject.org
173. OpenPaas - https://open-paas.org
174. Kolab Community - https://kolab.org
175. Gong - https://www.gong.io
176. Talkdesk - https://www.talkdesk.com
177. Aircall - https://aircall.io
178. Genesys - https://www.genesys.com
179. Cloudtalk - https://www.cloudtalk.io
180. Cireleloop - https://www.circleloop.com

181. eVoice - https://www.evoice.com
182. Squaretalk - https://squaretalk.com
183. Nextiva - https://www.nextiva.com
184. Workflowmax - https://www.workflowmax.com
185. Ganttpro - https://ganttpro.com
186. Mavenlink - https://www.mavenlink.com
187. Toggl - https://toggl.com
188. Celoxis - https://www.celoxis.com
189. Cmap - https://cmap.ihmc.us
190. HeySpace - https://hey.space
191. Pipedrive - https://www.pipedrive.com
192. Freshworks - https://www.freshworks.com
193. HubSpot CRM - https://www.hubspot.com
194. Salesforce - https://www.salesforce.com
195. Freshworks - https://www.freshworks.com
196. Mailchimp CRM - https://mailchimp.com
197. Proworkflow - https://www.proworkflow.com
198. Less Annoying CRM - https://www.lessannoyingcrm.com
199. Creatio - https://www.creatio.com
200. Benchmark CRM - https://www.benchmarkone.com
201. Really Simple Systems CRM - https://www.reallysimplesystems.com
202. InfoFlo CRM - https://infoflosolutions.com
203. Capsule CRM - https://capsulecrm.com
204. Engagebay CRM - https://www.engagebay.com
205. Odoo - https://www.odoo.com
206. OroCRM - https://oroinc.com/orocrm
207. X2CRM - https://x2crm.com
208. Vtiger CRM - https://www.vtiger.com
209. Espo CRM - https://www.espocrm.com
210. CiviCRM - https://civicrm.org
211. Streak - https://www.streak.com
212. SuiteCRM - https://suitecrm.com
213. Act CRM - https://www.act.com
214. Flowlu - https://www.flowlu.com
215. Salesflare - https://salesflare.com
216. Insightly CRM - https://www.insightly.com
217. Keap - https://keap.com
218. Alexor CRM - https://axelor.com/crm

219. Axonaut CRM - https://axonaut.com
220. Krayin CRM - https://krayincrm.com
221. Sugar CRM - https://www.sugarcrm.com
222. Corteza - https://cortezaproject.org
223. Yetiforce - https://yetiforce.com
224. Apache OFBiz - https://ofbiz.apache.org
225. Salesmate - https://www.salesmate.io
226. Oracle Netsuite - https://www.netsuite.com
227. Sage 300 - https://www.sage.com
228. Infor - https://www.infor.com
229. Strategic ERP - https://strategicerp.com
230. Syspro - https://asia.syspro.com
231. Deskera - https://www.deskera.com
232. Striven - https://www.striven.com
233. Katana ERP - https://katanamrp.com
234. ERPAG - https://www.erpag.com
235. OneHash - https://www.onehash.ai
236. WebERP - https://weberp.org
237. AccountMate - https://www.accountmate.com
238. Aptean - https://aptean.com
239. GreytHR - https://www.greythr.com
240. RazorPay Payroll - https://razorpay.com/payroll
241. Canopy - https://www.getcanopy.com
242. YayPay - https://www.yaypay.com
243. BigTime - https://www.bigtime.net
244. Accounting Seed - https://www.accountingseed.com
245. Freshbooks - https://www.freshbooks.com
246. Patriot ERP - https://www.patriotsoftware.com/accounting
247. Xero - https://www.xero.com
248. Wave Financial - https://www.waveapps.com
249. ZipBooks - https://zipbooks.com
250. Skrooge - https://skrooge.org
251. Akunting - https://akaunting.com
252. GNU Cash - https://www.gnucash.org
253. LedgerSMB - https://ledgersmb.org
254. Khatabook - https://khatabook.com
255. Quickbooks - https://quickbooks.intuit.com
256. Vyapar - https://vyaparapp.in

257. Busy Accounting - https://busy.in
258. ProfitBooks - https://www.profitbooks.net
259. Logic ERP - https://www.logicerp.com
260. MargERP - https://margcompusoft.com
261. ERPNext - https://erpnext.com
262. Tally ERP - https://tallysolutions.com
263. Ramco ERP - https://www.ramco.com/products/erp-software
264. SAP Business One - https://www.sap.com/products/erp/business-one.html
265. Dolibarr - https://www.dolibarr.org
266. Alexor - https://axelor.com
267. ERP5 - https://www.erp5.com
268. Metasfresh - https://metasfresh.com
269. xTuple - https://www.xtuple.com
270. SaplingHR - https://www.saplinghr.com
271. Containerize - https://www.containerize.com
272. Workday - https://www.workday.com
273. Deltek - https://www.deltek.com
274. Ukg - https://www.ukg.com
275. Epicor - https://www.epicor.com
276. PHP LIst - https://www.phplist.com
277. Mailwizz - https://www.mailwizz.com
278. Octeth - https://www2.octeth.com
279. Sendy - https://sendy.co
280. Mautic - https://www.mautic.org
281. Agnitas - https://www.agnitas.de
282. Moosend - https://moosend.com
283. Omnisend - https://www.omnisend.com
284. Sendinblue - https://www.sendinblue.com
285. Constant Contact - https://www.constantcontact.co
286. Aweber - https://www.aweber.com
287. Mailjet - https://www.mailjet.com
288. Zoho Campaigns - https://www.zoho.com/campaigns
289. Drip - https://www.drip.com
290. Listmonk - https://listmonk.app
291. Mailer Lite - https://www.mailerlite.com
292. SendPortal - https://sendportal.io
293. Adobe Workfront - https://www.workfront.com

294.   Microsoft Dynamics 365 - https://dynamics.microsoft.com
295.   Microsoft SharePoint - https://www.microsoft.com/en-us/microsoft-365/sharepoint/collaboration
296.   Microsoft Whiteboard - https://www.microsoft.com/en-us/microsoft-365/microsoft-whiteboard/digital-whiteboard-app

CHAPTER X

Content Tools

Grammar and Spelling Check, Language Translation, Transliteration, Plagiarism Checkers, Search Engine Optimisers (SEO), Digital Marketing Tools and Analytics, Paraphrasers, Backlinks, OCR, etc.

1. Scribbr - https://www.scribbr.com/plagiarism-checker
2. Copyscape - https://www.copyscape.com/compare.php
3. Google Transparency Report - https://transparencyreport.google.com
4. SmallSEOTools - https://smallseotools.com
5. Duplichecker - https://www.duplichecker.com
6. Grammarly - https://www.grammarly.com
7. ProWritingAid - https://prowritingaid.com
8. Jetpack - https://jetpack.com
9. LanguageTool - https://languagetool.org
10. Editsaurus - https://editsaurus.tylerwalters.com
11. Ginger Software - https://www.gingersoftware.com
12. Grammark - https://grammark.org
13. StoryToolz - https://storytoolz.com
14. Readable - https://readable.com
15. PaperRater - https://www.paperrater.com
16. Typopo - https://typopo.org
17. Grammar Lookup - https://www.grammarlookup.com
18. Espresso App - https://www.expresso-app.org
19. Duolingo - https://www.duolingo.com
20. Fluentify - https://www.fluentify.com
21. Hello English - https://helloenglish.com
22. Worddive -https://www.worddive.com
23. Transparent Language - https://www.transparent.com
24. Pre Post SEO - https://www.prepostseo.com
25. Google Translate - https://translate.google.com
26. Microsoft Translator - https://translator.microsoft.com
27. Amazon Translate -https://aws.amazon.com/translate
28. IBM AI tools - https://www.ibm.com/cloud/ai
29. Yandex Translate - https://translate.yandex.com

30. Outwrite - https://www.outwrite.com
31. Orfogrammka - https://orfogrammka.ru
32. Reverso - https://www.reverso.net/text-translation
33. Writer - https://writer.com
34. Eangel - https://www.eangel.me
35. iTranslate - https://www.itranslate.com
36. Typeright - https://typeright.com
37. Linguee - https://www.linguee.com
38. Babylon Translator - https://www.babylon-software.com
39. Online transliteration - https://the-translit.com
40. Smartcat - https://www.smartcat.com
41. Memsource - https://www.memsource.com
42. Wordbee - https://www.wordbee.com
43. Omegat - https://omegat.org
44. Matecat - https://www.matecat.com
45. DeepL Translator - https://www.deepl.com/translator
46. XTM Cloud - https://xtm.cloud
47. Google Search Console - https://search.google.com/search-console/about
48. Internetmarketingninjas - https://www.internetmarketingninjas.com
49. Woorank - https://www.woorank.com
50. SpyFu - https://www.spyfu.com
51. Semrush - https://www.semrush.com
52. Mangools - https://mangools.com
53. Ahrefs - https://ahrefs.com
54. Answer The Public - https://answerthepublic.com
55. Ubersuggest - https://neilpatel.com/ubersuggest
56. Majestic - https://majestic.com
57. Google Trends - https://trends.google.com
58. Seoquake - https://www.seoquake.com
59. Siteliner - https://siteliner.com
60. Screaming Frog SEO - https://www.screamingfrog.co.uk/seo-spider
61. Serpstat - https://serpstat.com
62. Google Page Speed Insights - https://pagespeed.web.dev
63. Microsoft Bing Webmaster - https://www.bing.com/webmasters/about
64. Google Analytics - https://analytics.google.com
65. Yoast SEO - https://yoast.com
66. Similar Web - https://www.similarweb.com

67. ClearWebStats - https://www.clearwebstats.com
68. Digital Point - https://tools.digitalpoint.com
69. Ispionage - https://www.ispionage.com
70. Nibbler - https://nibbler.insites.com
71. Pageglimpse - https://www.pageglimpse.org
72. Quicksprout - https://www.quicksprout.com
73. SEO Site Checkup - https://seositecheckup.com
74. Hypestat - https://hypestat.com
75. Shodan - https://www.shodan.io
76. Website Informer - https://website.informer.com
77. Websiteoutlook - https://websiteoutlook.com
78. WebPageTest - https://www.webpagetest.org
79. Statvoo - https://statvoo.com
80. Statscrop - https://www.statscrop.com
81. XML Sitemaps - https://www.xml-sitemaps.com
82. Keywords Everywhere - https://keywordseverywhere.com
83. Linkody - https://www.linkody.com
84. Finder - https://finder.app
85. Site Report - https://sitereport.netcraft.com
86. Buildwith - https://builtwith.com
87. Open Link Profiler - https://www.openlinkprofiler.org
88. URL Scan - https://urlscan.io
89. Blue Backlinks - https://bluebacklinks.com
90. Moz Pro - https://moz.com
91. i2OCR - https://www.i2ocr.com
92. Image Translate - https://www.imagetranslate.com
93. iSolid - https://www.isolid.be
94. New OCR - https://www.newocr.com
95. Online OCR - https://www.onlineocr.net
96. Project Naptha - https://projectnaptha.com
97. SimpleOCR - https://www.simpleocr.com
98. Nanonets - https://nanonets.com
99. Easy Screen OCR - https://easyscreenocr.com

CHAPTER XI

Security + Privacy

Data and Device Security, Safety and Privacy, Password Management, Secure Login, Compliance, Legal Assurance, Cyber Security, etc.

1. Malwarebytes - https://www.malwarebytes.com
2. No More Ransom - https://www.nomoreransom.org/en/index.html
3. Apple iFind - https://www.apple.com/icloud/find-my
4. HiddenApp - https://hiddenapp.com
5. Lookout - https://www.lookout.com
6. Prey Project - https://preyproject.com
7. Home Office - https://homeoffice.absolute.com
8. Microsoft Security - https://www.microsoft.com/en-us/security
9. Authy - https://authy.com
10. 1Password - https://1password.com
11. Bitwarden - https://bitwarden.com
12. Dashlane - https://www.dashlane.com
13. LastPass - https://www.lastpass.com
14. Passbolt - https://www.passbolt.com
15. BrainStation - https://brainstation.io
16. Yubico - https://www.yubico.com
17. LessPass - https://www.lesspass.com
18. Google Authentication - https://safety.google/authentication
19. Siteimprove - https://www.siteimprove.com
20. Accessible - https://accessibe.com
21. Deque - https://www.deque.com
22. Drata - https://drata.com/
23. Securwires - https://securwires.com/about-us.php
24. Commugen - https://www.cyber.commugen.com
25. CyberGRX - https://www.cybergrx.com
26. Cye - https://cyesec.com
27. Secureframe - https://secureframe.com
28. Security Scorecard - https://securityscorecard.com
29. NewSoftwares - https://www.newsoftwares.net
30. Convercent - https://www.convercent.com

31. Brinqa - https://www.brinqa.com
32. Safe - https://www.safe.security
33. Sentilink - https://www.sentilink.com
34. Hicomply - https://hicomply.com
35. Panorays - https://panorays.com
36. Heylaika - https://heylaika.com
37. Socure - https://www.socure.com
38. Controlmap - https://www.controlmap.io
39. Travasecurity - https://www.travasecurity.com
40. Change Detect - https://www.changedetect.com
41. Hyperproof - https://hyperproof.io
42. RFP360 - https://rfp360.com
43. Loopio - https://loopio.com
44. Audit Board - https://www.auditboard.com
45. Sprinto - https://sprinto.com
46. Tugboat Logic - https://tugboatlogic.com
47. Vanta - https://www.vanta.com
48. Solarwinds - https://www.solarwinds.com
49. UpGuard - https://www.upguard.com
50. Recuva - https://www.ccleaner.com/recuva
51. Trackly - https://trackly.io
52. DigiKam - https://www.digikam.org

CHAPTER XII

Learning Management Systems

Education, Learning, Virtual Engagement Tools, Training, MOOC, Skill Development, Surveys, Forms, etc.

1. OpenLMS - https://www.openlms.net
2. Absorb LMS - https://www.absorblms.com
3. ProProfs - https://www.proprofs.com
4. iSpring LMS - https://www.ispringsolutions.com
5. TalentLMS - https://www.talentlms.com
6. Docebo - https://www.docebo.com
7. Adobe Captivate Prime LMS - https://www.adobe.com/products/captivateprime.html
8. PowerSchool - https://www.powerschool.com
9. Quizlet - https://quizlet.com
10. GoSkills - https://www.goskills.com
11. Moodle - https://moodle.org
12. Dokeos - https://www.dokeos.com
13. Open edX - https://openedx.org
14. Chamil LMS - https://chamilo.org
15. Odoo LMS - https://www.odoo.com/app/elearning
16. Google Classroom - https://classroom.google.com
17. Sakai LMS - https://www.sakailms.org
18. OpenOLAT - https://www.openolat.com
19. ATutor - https://atutor.github.io
20. ILIAS LMS - https://www.ilias.de
21. Coggno LMS - https://coggno.com
22. Opigno LMS - https://www.drupal.org/project/opigno_lms
23. Skyprep LMS - https://skyprep.com
24. Eduflow LMS - https://www.eduflow.com
25. Easy LMS - https://www.easy-lms.com
26. SAP Litmos LMS - https://www.litmos.com
27. Learnupon LMS - https://www.learnupon.com
28. Forma LMS - https://formalms.org
29. D2L - https://www.d2l.com

30. Cypher Learning Matrix - https://www.cypherlearning.com/matrix
31. AhaSlides - https://ahaslides.com
32. Quizizz - https://quizizz.com
33. Slido - https://www.slido.com
34. QuestionPro - https://www.questionpro.com
35. Mentimeter - https://www.mentimeter.com
36. Slido - https://www.slido.com
37. Poll Everywhere - https://www.polleverywhere.com
38. MyQuiz - https://myquiz.org
39. Kahoot - https://kahoot.it
40. Google Forms - https://docs.google.com/forms
41. Microsoft Forms - https://forms.microsoft.com
42. Forms - https://forms.io
43. Jotform - https://www.jotform.com
44. Paperform - https://paperform.co
45. Formstack - https://www.formstack.com
46. 123 Form Builder - https://www.123formbuilder.com
47. Hubspot Forms - https://www.hubspot.com/products/marketing/forms
48. Zoho Forms - https://www.zoho.com/forms
49. Gravity Forms - https://www.gravityforms.com
50. Formsite - https://www.formsite.com
51. WPForms - https://wpforms.com
52. Cognito Forms - https://www.cognitoforms.com
53. Ninja Forms - https://ninjaforms.com
54. Typeform - https://www.typeform.com
55. OhMyForm - https://ohmyform.com
56. Form Tools - https://formtools.org
57. Budibase - https://budibase.com
58. Wufoo - https://www.wufoo.com
59. SurveySparrow - https://surveysparrow.com
60. SurveyMonkey - https://www.surveymonkey.com
61. SuperSurvey - https://www.supersurvey.com
62. SoGoSurvey - https://www.sogosurvey.com
63. Survicate - https://survicate.com
64. Qualtrics - https://www.qualtrics.com
65. Survey Legend - https://www.surveylegend.com
66. Alchemer - https://www.alchemer.com

67. SurveyPlanet - https://surveyplanet.com
68. Survs - https://survs.com
69. LimeSurvey - https://www.limesurvey.org
70. Kwik Surveys - https://kwiksurveys.com
71. ngSurvey - https://www.ngsurvey.com
72. TellForm - https://www.tellform.com
73. Coursera - https://www.coursera.org
74. Udacity - https://www.udacity.com
75. Udemy - https://www.udemy.com
76. Mooc - https://www.mooc.org
77. Khan Academy - https://www.khanacademy.org
78. Canvas - https://www.canvas.net
79. FutureLearn - https://www.futurelearn.com
80. The Open University - https://www.open.ac.uk
81. Thinkific - https://www.thinkific.com
82. Alison - https://alison.com
83. Domestika - https://www.domestika.org
84. Skillshare - https://www.skillshare.com
85. Codecademy - https://www.codecademy.com
86. Cognitive Class - https://cognitiveclass.ai
87. LinkedIn Learning - https://www.linkedin.com/learning
88. MIT OCW - https://ocw.mit.edu
89. Swayam - https://swayam.gov.in
90. Open Learning - https://www.openlearning.com
91. OpenClassrooms - https://openclassrooms.com
92. Shaw Academy - https://www.shawacademy.com
93. Open HPI - https://open.hpi.de
94. Datacamp - https://www.datacamp.com
95. BitDegree - https://www.bitdegree.org
96. NAS Academy - https://nasacademy.com
97. Edureka - https://www.edureka.co
98. Simplilearn - https://www.simplilearn.com
99. NovoEd - https://www.novoed.com
100. Iversity - https://iversity.org

CHAPTER XIII

Video + Graphics + Animation

Editing, Conversion, Compression, 2D & 3D Graphic Modelling, Simulation and Animation Applications, etc.

1. Blender - https://www.blender.org
2. DaVinci Resolve - https://www.blackmagicdesign.com/products/davinciresolve
3. Fusion - https://www.blackmagicdesign.com/products/fusion
4. Adobe Animate - https://www.adobe.com/products/animate.html
5. Adobe After Effects - https://www.adobe.com/products/aftereffects.html
6. Adobe Premiere Pro - https://www.adobe.com/products/premiere.html
7. Adobe Media Encoder - https://www.adobe.com/products/media-encoder.html
8. Adobe Character - https://www.adobe.com/products/character-animator.html
9. Renderforest - https://www.renderforest.com
10. Videoscribe - https://www.videoscribe.co
11. Cyberlink - https://www.cyberlink.com
12. Clipchamp - https://clipchamp.com
13. YouTube Studio - https://studio.youtube.com
14. Vimeo - https://vimeo.com
15. Kinemaster - https://kinemaster.com
16. GoPro - https://gopro.com
17. InShot - https://www.inshot.com
18. Splice - https://www.spliceapp.com
19. Filmora Wondershare - https://filmora.wondershare.com
20. Videostudio - https://www.videostudiopro.com
21. Pinnacle Studio - https://www.pinnaclesys.com
22. Magisto - https://www.magisto.com
23. Movavi - https://www.movavi.com
24. Krita - https://krita.org
25. Pencil 2D - https://www.pencil2d.org
26. Synfig - https://www.synfig.org

27. Rawshorts - https://www.rawshorts.com
28. Vyond - https://www.vyond.com
29. Animaker - https://www.animaker.com
30. Doodly - https://www.doodly.com
31. Toonly - https://www.toonly.com
32. Promo - https://promo.com
33. Visme - https://www.visme.co
34. WeVideo - https://www.wevideo.com
35. MSFT Editor https://www.microsoft.com/en-us/windows/photo-movie-editor
36. VLC Media - https://www.videolan.org/vlc
37. MPV - https://mpv.io
38. Kdenlive - https://kdenlive.org
39. Openshot Video Editor - https://www.openshot.org
40. VideoPad - https://www.nchsoftware.com/videopad
41. VSDC Video Editor - https://www.videosoftdev.com
42. Apple iMovie Editor - https://www.apple.com/imovie
43. Apple Clips - https://www.apple.com/clips
44. Apple Final Cut Pro - https://www.apple.com/final-cut-pro
45. Cisdem - https://www.cisdem.com
46. Flexclip - https://www.flexclip.com
47. Kdenlive - https://kdenlive.org
48. Opentoonz - https://opentoonz.github.io
49. Handbrake Video Transcoder - https://handbrake.fr
50. Videoproc - https://www.videoproc.com
51. Ashampoo - https://www.ashampoo.com
52. Kapwing - https://www.kapwing.com
53. Rocketium - https://rocketium.com
54. Powtoon - https://www.powtoon.com
55. Clideo - https://clideo.com
56. Animoto - https://animoto.com
57. Wave - https://wave.video
58. Typito - https://typito.com/
59. Wideo - https://wideo.co
60. Media - https://www.media.io
61. Ffmpeg - https://ffmpeg.org
62. Keepvid - https://keepvid.com
63. Kizoa - https://www.kizoa.com

64. Maxon - https://www.maxon.net
65. Foundry - https://www.foundry.com
66. LWKS - https://lwks.com
67. Magix - https://www.magix.com
68. Media 100 - https://www.media100.com
69. Nero - https://www.nero.com
70. Shotcut - https://shotcut.org
71. Natron - https://natrongithub.github.io
72. Cgtrader - https://www.cgtrader.com
73. HitFilm FX Home - https://fxhome.com
74. Sidefx - https://www.sidefx.com
75. Nextlimit RealFlow - https://realflow.com
76. Olive Video Editor - https://www.olivevideoeditor.org
77. Autodesk Maya - https://www.autodesk.com/products/maya
78. Natron - https://natrongithub.github.io
79. Daz 3D - https://www.daz3d.com
80. BRL CAD - https://brlcad.org
81. FreeCAD - https://www.freecad.org
82. Libre CAD - https://librecad.org
83. AliceVision - https://alicevision.org
84. 3D Export - https://3dexport.com
85. 3D Warehouse - https://3dwarehouse.sketchup.com
86. Cults3D - https://cults3d.com
87. 3D Warehouse - https://3dwarehouse.sketchup.com
88. Cgtrader - https://www.cgtrader.com
89. GrabCAD - https://grabcad.com
90. Thingiverse - https://www.thingiverse.com
91. Turbosquid - https://www.turbosquid.com
92. MyMiniFactory - https://www.myminifactory.com
93. Yeggi - https://www.yeggi.com
94. Turbosquid - https://www.turbosquid.com
95. Thingiverse - https://www.thingiverse.com
96. Sketchfab - https://sketchfab.com
97. Pinshape - https://pinshape.com
98. Clara - https://clara.io
99. OpenToonz - https://opentoonz.github.io
100. GIMP - https://www.gimp.org
101. Flowblade - https://jliljebl.github.io/flowblade

102. Offeo - https://offeo.com
103. Sony Vegas Pro - https://www.vegascreativesoftware.com
104. Clipify - https://clipify.net
105. VEED - https://www.veed.io
106. Fastreel - https://www.fastreel.com
107. Studiobinder - https://www.studiobinder.com
108. Toonboom - https://www.toonboom.com
109. Reallusion - https://www.reallusion.com
110. Cateater - https://www.cateater.com
111. Planetside - https://planetside.co.uk
112. Flipsnack - https://www.flipsnack.com
113. Avid - https://www.avid.com
114. Canva Video Editor - https://www.canva.com/create/photo-videos
115. Any Video Converter - https://www.any-video-converter.com
116. Freemake Video Convertor - https://www.freemake.com
117. CloudConvert - https://cloudconvert.com
118. Divx - https://in.divx.com
119. MiniTool Video Convertor - https://videoconvert.minitool.com
120. Acdsee - https://www.acdsee.com
121. Online Convert - https://www.online-convert.com

CHAPTER XIV

Audio + Music

Editing and Mastering Studio Tools, Speech to Text, Text to Speech, Music Production, etc.

1. Adobe Audition - https://www.adobe.com/products/audition.html
2. Avid Pro Tools - https://www.avid.com/pro-tools
3. Presonus - https://www.presonus.com
4. Audacity - https://www.audacityteam.org
5. Steinberg Cubase - https://www.steinberg.net
6. Magix - https://www.magix.com
7. Ocenaudio - https://www.ocenaudio.com
8. Ashampoo - https://www.ashampoo.com
9. Reaper - https://www.reaper.fm
10. Acoustica - https://acoustica.com
11. Free Audio Editor - https://free-audio-editor.com
12. Ableton - https://www.ableton.com
13. FL Studio - https://www.image-line.com
14. Acon Digital - https://acondigital.com
15. Audiotool - https://www.audiotool.com
16. Rogueamoeba - https://rogueamoeba.com
17. Hindenburg - https://hindenburg.com
18. Mp3 Cut - https://mp3cut.net
19. Narration Box - https://narrationbox.com
20. Qtractor - https://qtractor.org
21. Soundation - https://soundation.com
22. Spext - https://www.spext.co
23. Twisted Wave - https://twistedwave.com
24. Wavepad - https://www.nch.com.au/wavepad
25. Drafts - https://getdrafts.com
26. Dictation - https://dictation.io
27. Otter - https://otter.ai
28. Sonix - https://sonix.ai
29. Speechmatics - https://www.speechmatics.com
30. Google Speech to text - https://cloud.google.com/speech-to-text

31. Microsoft Azure Speech to text - https://azure.microsoft.com
32. Amazon Transcribe - https://aws.amazon.com/transcribe
33. Speechnotes - https://speechnotes.co
34. Joplin - https://joplinapp.org
35. Simplenote - https://simplenote.com
36. Standard Notes - https://standardnotes.com
37. Speechtexter - https://www.speechtexter.com
38. Trint - https://trint.com
39. Verbit - https://verbit.ai
40. IBM Watson - https://www.ibm.com/cloud/watson-speech-to-text
41. Captivoice - https://www.captivoice.com
42. Hearling - https://hearling.com
43. Text to Speech - https://www.ispeech.org
44. Kukarella - https://www.kukarella.com
45. Linguatec - https://www.linguatec.de
46. Lexis Audio Editor - https://www.lexisaudioeditor.com
47. GarageBand - https://www.apple.com/ios/garageband
48. Audiomass - https://audiomass.co
49. LMMS - https://lmms.io
50. Ardour - https://ardour.org
51. Akaipro - https://www.akaipro.com
52. Trackiton - https://www.tracktion.com
53. SoundBridge - https://soundbridge.io
54. Bandlab - https://www.bandlab.com
55. Avid Pro Tools- https://www.avid.com
56. Soundtrap - https://www.soundtrap.com
57. Serato - https://serato.com
58. Soundstation Studio - https://soundation.com
59. Mixxx - https://mixxx.org
60. Mulab - https://www.mutools.com
61. MusE - https://muse-sequencer.github.io
62. Ordrumbox - https://www.ordrumbox.com
63. Reason Studios - https://reasonstudios.com
64. Ninja Jamm - https://www.ninjajamm.com
65. Loudly - https://www.loudly.com
66. Otranscribe - https://otranscribe.com
67. Amazon Alexa - https://alexa.amazon.com
68. Google Assistant - https://assistant.google.com

69. Apple Siri - https://www.apple.com/siri
70. Microsoft Cortana - https://www.microsoft.com/en-us/cortana

CHAPTER XV

Photos + Creative Assets

Photograph Editing, Designing Apps, Digital Flyer and Poster Makers, Stock Images, Illustrations, Vector Artworks, GIFs, Icons, Resizers, PDF Editors and Convertors, E-Sign, Barcode, QR Code Generator and Digital Scanners, Document Management Systems, etc.

1. Adobe Lightroom - https://www.adobe.com/products/photoshop-lightroom.html
2. Adobe Photoshop - https://www.adobe.com/products/photoshop.html
3. Adobe Express - https://www.adobe.com/express
4. Adobe Illustrator - https://www.adobe.com/products/illustrator.html
5. GIMP - https://www.gimp.org
6. CorelDRAW - https://www.coreldraw.com
7. Photodirector - https://www.cyberlink.com
8. DxO Shop - https://shop.dxo.com
9. Capture One - https://www.captureone.com
10. Syklum Luminar - https://skylum.com/luminar
11. Acdsee - https://www.acdsee.com
12. Pixlr - https://pixlr.com
13. Movavi Pic Verse - https://www.movavi.com/photo-editor
14. Internetmarketingninjas - https://www.internetmarketingninjas.com
15. BeFunky - https://www.befunky.com
16. Canva - https://www.canva.com
17. Affinity - https://affinity.serif.com
18. Exposure - https://exposure.software
19. Fotor - https://www.fotor.com
20. Pizap - https://www.pizap.com
21. ON1 - https://www.on1.com
22. Picozu - https://www.picozu.com
23. Photopea - https://www.photopea.com
24. Editor Photo - https://editor.pho.to
25. RawTherapee - https://rawtherapee.com
26. DigiKam - https://www.digikam.org
27. Pixen - https://pixenapp.com

28. Inkscape - https://inkscape.org
29. Krita - https://krita.org
30. Darktable - https://www.darktable.org
31. Photovio - https://photivo.org
32. ImageOptim - https://imageoptim.com
33. Pinta - https://www.pinta-project.com
34. Piktochart - https://piktochart.com
35. Postermywall - https://www.postermywall.com
36. MyCreativeShop - https://www.mycreativeshop.com
37. Desygner - https://desygner.com
38. GraphicSprings - https://www.graphicsprings.com
39. Blockposters - https://www.blockposters.com
40. Drawtify - https://drawtify.com
41. Visme - https://www.visme.co
42. Stencil - https://getstencil.com
43. Vista - https://create.vista.com
44. Design Cap - https://www.designcap.com
45. Adobe Stock - https://stock.adobe.com
46. Picjumbo - https://picjumbo.com
47. Foodiesfeed - https://www.foodiesfeed.com
48. Reshot - https://www.reshot.com
49. Moose - https://icons8.com
50. Getty Images - https://www.gettyimages.in
51. Image Finder - https://imagefinder.co
52. Burst - https://burst.shopify.com
53. IM creator - https://www.imcreator.com
54. Gratisography - https://gratisography.com
55. MorgueFile - https://morguefile.com
56. FOCA Stock - https://focastock.com
57. Negative Space - https://negativespace.co
58. Free Images - https://www.freeimages.com
59. Piqsels - https://www.piqsels.com
60. Free Nature Stock - https://freenaturestock.com
61. Public Domain Archive - https://publicdomainarchive.com
62. Kaboompics - https://kaboompics.com
63. SplitShire - https://www.splitshire.com
64. Pikwizard - https://pikwizard.com
65. Skitterphoto - https://skitterphoto.com

66. iStock - https://www.istockphoto.com
67. Librestock - https://librestock.com
68. Vecteezy - https://www.vecteezy.com
69. Pixelmob - https://pixelmob.co
70. Shutterstock - https://www.shutterstock.com
71. ISO Republic - https://isorepublic.com
72. Picography - https://picography.co
73. Freestocks - https://freestocks.org
74. Shostash - https://shotstash.com
75. Pixabay - https://pixabay.com
76. Little Visuals - https://littlevisuals.co
77. Clipstill - https://www.clipstill.com
78. Openverse - https://wordpress.org/openverse
79. Stocksnap - https://stocksnap.io
80. Unsplash - https://unsplash.com
81. Photobucket - https://photobucket.com
82. Pexels - https://www.pexels.com
83. Life Of Pix - https://www.lifeofpix.com
84. Styledstock - https://styledstock.co
85. Startupstockphotos - https://startupstockphotos.com
86. AllTheFreeStock - https://allthefreestock.com
87. AddText - https://addtext.com
88. Snapseed - https://snapseedpc.com
89. Polarr - https://www.polarr.com
90. Pinkmirror - https://pinkmirror.com
91. Removebg - https://www.remove.bg
92. XnView - https://www.xnview.com
93. ZapBG - https://zapbg.com
94. Birme - https://www.birme.net
95. Artbreeder - https://www.artbreeder.com
96. BatchPhoto - https://www.batchphoto.com
97. Blurity - https://www.blurity.com
98. Singularlabs - https://singularlabs.com
99. Fotoflexer - https://fotoflexer.com
100. Let's Enhance - https://letsenhance.io
101. High Motion - https://www.highmotionsoftware.com
102. Image Enlarger - https://www.imageenlarger.com
103. Online Convert - https://onlineconvertfree.com

104.   Picmonkey - https://www.picmonkey.com
105.   Optimage - https://optimage.app
106.   Photovisi - https://www.photovisi.com
107.   Buffer - https://buffer.com
108.   Photofunny - https://www.photofunny.net
109.   Make Photo Gallery - https://makephotogallery.net
110.   Photojoiner - https://www.photojoiner.net
111.   TheXifer - https://www.thexifer.net
112.   Ezgif - https://ezgif.com
113.   Photo Scissors - https://photoscissors.com
114.   TinyPNG - https://tinypng.com
115.   Promo - https://promo.com
116.   Sumo - https://sumo.app
117.   Soda PDF - https://www.sodapdf.com
118.   Adobe Acrobat - https://acrobat.adobe.com
119.   OmniPage Kofax - https://www.kofax.com
120.   PDF Abbyy - https://pdf.abbyy.com
121.   Microsoft OneNote - https://www.onenote.com
122.   Amazon Textract - https://aws.amazon.com/textract
123.   Google Docs - https://docs.google.com
124.   Rossum - https://rossum.ai
125.   Wondershare PDF - https://pdf.wondershare.com
126.   Datamolino - https://www.datamolino.com
127.   Sejda - https://www.sejda.com
128.   Irislink - https://www.irislink.com
129.   PDFescape - https://www.pdfescape.com
130.   Smallpdf - https://smallpdf.com
131.   LibreOffice Draw - https://www.libreoffice.org
132.   PDFbob - https://pdfbob.com
133.   Pdfpen - https://pdfpen.com
134.   Pdf Candy - https://pdfcandy.com
135.   Aconvert - https://www.aconvert.com
136.   PDF Convertor - https://www.freepdfconvert.com
137.   PDFonFly - https://pdfonfly.com
138.   Investintech - https://www.investintech.com
139.   PDFYeah - https://www.pdfyeah.com
140.   PublishertoPDF - https://www.publishertopdf.com
141.   Tracker Software - https://www.tracker-software.com

142. ScanDoc - https://scandoc.io
143. VueScan - https://www.hamrick.com
144. PaperScan - https://paperscan.orpalis.com
145. Adobe QR Generator - https://www.adobe.com/express/feature/image/qr-code-generator
146. QR Code Generator - https://www.qr-code-generator.com
147. QRCode Monkey - https://www.qrcode-monkey.com
148. Beaconstac QR - https://www.beaconstac.com/qr-code-generator
149. Scanova - https://scanova.io
150. Shopify QR Generator - https://www.shopify.com/tools/qr-code-generator
151. QRstuff - https://www.qrstuff.com
152. Unitag QR - https://www.unitag.io
153. uQR - https://uqr.me
154. QRTiger - https://www.qrcode-tiger.com
155. GoQR - https://goqr.me
156. ZebraQR - https://www.zebra-qr.com
157. Delivr QR - https://delivr.com
158. Visme - https://www.visme.co
159. Pageloot - https://pageloot.com
160. QR scanner - https://www.qrscanner.org
161. Scandit - https://www.scandit.com
162. Apple QR Scanner - https://support.apple.com/en-us/HT208843
163. Barcode Scanner - https://barcodescanr.com
164. Adobe Scanner - https://www.adobe.com/acrobat/mobile/scanner-app.html
165. Openkm - https://www.openkm.com
166. Kimios - https://www.kimios.com
167. Bitrix24 - https://www.bitrix24.in
168. PandaDoc - https://www.pandadoc.com
169. Nuxeo - https://www.nuxeo.com
170. M-Files - https://www.m-files.com

CHAPTER XVI

Storage + Sharing

Encryption, Sync, File Sharing, Cloud Computing Applications, etc.

1. Google Drive - https://drive.google.com
2. Dropbox - https://www.dropbox.com
3. Microsoft Onedrive - https://onedrive.com
4. Mega - https://mega.io
5. iDrive - https://www.idrive.com
6. Sync - https://www.sync.com
7. Box - https://www.box.com
8. MediaFire - https://www.mediafire.com
9. Backblaze - https://www.backblaze.com
10. Carbonite - https://www.carbonite.com
11. CloudApp - https://www.getcloudapp.com
12. Cloudfuze - https://www.cloudfuze.com
13. Zoolz - https://www.zoolz.com
14. WeTransfer - https://wetransfer.com
15. Transfer Big Files - https://www.transferbigfiles.com
16. Simple Savr - https://www.ssavr.com
17. CloudHQ - https://www.cloudhq.net
18. Send This File - https://www.sendthisfile.com
19. DropSend - https://www.dropsend.com
20. GoogSync - https://www.goodsync.com
21. Zoho WorkDrive - https://www.zoho.com/workdrive
22. Hightail - https://www.hightail.com
23. Live Drive - https://www2.livedrive.com
24. MultCloud - https://www.multcloud.com
25. Egnyte - https://www.egnyte.com
26. Onehub - https://www.onehub.com
27. Hubic - https://hubic.com
28. pCloud - https://www.pcloud.com
29. Send Anywhere - https://send-anywhere.com
30. Tresorit - https://tresorit.com
31. Idgard - https://www.idgard.com

32. OwnCloud - https://owncloud.com
33. Degoo - https://degoo.com
34. Yandex Disk - https://disk.yandex.com
35. Blomp - https://www.blomp.com
36. Internxt - https://internxt.com
37. Icedrive - https://icedrive.net
38. Jumpshare - https://jumpshare.com
39. Terabox - https://www.terabox.com
40. Boxcryptor - https://www.boxcryptor.com
41. Pydio - https://pydio.com
42. Seafile - https://www.seafile.com
43. Ceph - https://ceph.io
44. Xigmanas - https://xigmanas.com
45. Syncthing - https://syncthing.net
46. Cozy Cloud - https://cozy.io
47. YouTransfer - https://www.youtransfer.io
48. Tonido - https://www.tonido.com
49. Koofr - https://koofr.eu
50. SpiderOak - https://spideroak.com
51. Cryptomator - https://cryptomator.org
52. Apple iCloud - https://www.apple.com/icloud
53. Amazon Cloud Drive - https://www.amazon.com/clouddrive
54. IBM Cloud - https://cloud.ibm.com
55. Alibaba Cloud - https://in.alibabacloud.com
56. Red Hat Cloud - https://cloud.redhat.com
57. Google Cloud - https://cloud.google.com
58. Oracle Cloud - https://www.oracle.com/cloud
59. Microsoft Azure - https://azure.microsoft.com
60. Amazon Web Services - https://aws.amazon.com
61. NetApp Cloud - https://cloud.netapp.com
62. Gcore Labs - https://gcorelabs.com
63. Dplyr - https://www.dplyr.dev
64. OpenStack - https://www.openstack.org
65. Apache CloudStack - https://cloudstack.apache.org
66. Eucalyptus - https://www.eucalyptus.cloud
67. OpenQRM - https://openqrm-enterprise.com
68. Airdrop - https://support.apple.com/en-us/HT204144
69. Smart Transfer - https://www.smarttransferapp.com

70. AirDroid - https://www.airdroid.com
71. Pushbullet - https://www.pushbullet.com
72. FileZilla - https://filezilla-project.org
73. TrueNAS - https://www.truenas.com

CHAPTER XVII

Web Tools

Web Development Apps, Optimisation, Text and Code Editors, CMS App-Game Builders, Store Creators, Marketing Content Generator, Payment Gateways, Blog Platforms, Code Repositories, Domain and Hosting Platforms, UI/UX, Wireframe Tools, Testing Platforms, Servers, URL Shorteners, etc.

1. WordPress - https://wordpress.com
2. Drupal - https://www.drupal.org
3. Wix - https://www.wix.com
4. Joomla - https://www.joomla.org
5. Zoho Sites - https://www.zoho.com/sites/website-builder.html
6. Shopify Website Builder - https://www.shopify.com/website/builder
7. Adobe Business - https://business.adobe.com
8. UltraEdit - https://www.ultraedit.com
9. Overwolf - https://www.overwolf.com
10. Boldgrid - https://www.boldgrid.com
11. Duda - https://www.duda.co
12. Tilda - https://tilda.cc
13. Ghost - https://ghost.org
14. IM Creator - https://www.imcreator.com
15. WebStarts - https://www.webstarts.com
16. Jimdo - https://www.jimdo.com
17. GoDaddy - https://www.godaddy.com/en-ca/websites/website-builder
18. Website Builder - https://www.websitebuilder.com
19. Yola - https://www.yola.com
20. Weebly - https://www.weebly.com
21. Simvoly - https://simvoly.com
22. Webnode - https://us.webnode.com
23. Web - https://www.web.com
24. Sitebuilder - https://www.sitebuilder.com
25. Google Sites - https://workspace.google.com/products/sites
26. Webflow - https://webflow.com
27. Sitey - https://www.sitey.com

28. Ucraft - https://www.ucraft.com
29. SquareSpace - https://www.squarespace.com
30. Sheet2Site - https://www.sheet2site.com
31. Firepad - https://firepad.io
32. Strikingly - https://www.strikingly.com
33. Ucoz - https://www.ucoz.com
34. Voog - https://www.voog.com
35. Ukit - https://ukit.com
36. Webiny - https://www.webiny.com
37. Unstack - https://www.unstack.com
38. Snaplitics - https://snaplitics.com
39. Microweber - https://microweber.org
40. Publii - https://getpublii.com
41. Silex - https://www.silex.me
42. GrapeJS - https://grapesjs.com
43. Subrion - https://subrion.org
44. Modx - https://modx.com
45. BuilderEngine - https://builderengine.com
46. Django CMS - https://www.django-cms.org
47. ConcreteCMS - https://www.concretecms.com
48. Ecwid - https://www.ecwid.com
49. Square - https://squareup.com
50. CS Cart - https://www.cs-cart.com
51. NopCommerce - https://www.nopcommerce.com
52. OpenCart - https://www.opencart.com
53. Bitrix24 - https://www.bitrix24.com
54. Silverstripe - https://www.silverstripe.org
55. Liferay - https://www.liferay.com
56. Prestashop - https://www.prestashop.com
57. Orchardcore - https://orchardcore.net
58. Google Pay - https://pay.google.com
59. Intuit - https://www.intuit.com
60. Taler - https://taler.net
61. PayPal - https://www.paypal.com
62. Wise - https://wise.com
63. Razorpay - https://razorpay.com
64. Stripe - https://stripe.com
65. Authorize - https://www.authorize.net

66. Braintree - https://www.braintreepayments.com
67. WePay - https://go.wepay.com
68. 2Checkout - https://www.2checkout.com
69. Staxpayments - https://staxpayments.com
70. Helcim - https://www.helcim.com
71. Clover - https://www.clover.com
72. Payment Cloud - https://paymentcloudinc.com
73. Adyen - https://www.adyen.com
74. Unipay - https://unipaygateway.com
75. Medium - https://medium.com
76. Blogger - https://www.blogger.com
77. LinkedIn - https://www.linkedin.com
78. HubSpot - https://www.hubspot.com/products/marketing/blog
79. Peppertype - https://www.peppertype.ai
80. Red Points - https://www.redpoints.com
81. ClosersCopy - https://www.closerscopy.com
82. Jasper - https://www.jasper.ai
83. Writesonic - https://writesonic.com
84. Copy - https://www.copy.ai
85. Any Word - https://anyword.com
86. Hootsuite - https://www.hootsuite.com
87. Copysmith - https://copysmith.ai
88. Write - https://write.as
89. Tumblr - https://www.tumblr.com
90. Jekyll - https://jekyllrb.com
91. Hexo - https://hexo.io
92. Appery - https://appery.io
93. Zoho App Creator - https://www.zoho.com/creator
94. Sell My App - https://www.sellmyapp.com
95. Brackets - https://brackets.io
96. GNU Emacs - https://www.gnu.org/software/emacs
97. Bootstrap - https://getbootstrap.com
98. Ruby on Rails - https://rubyonrails.org
99. Eclipse - https://www.eclipse.org
100. NetBeans - https://netbeans.apache.org
101. Godotengine - https://godotengine.org
102. GDevelop - https://gdevelop.io
103. Game Maker - https://gamemaker.io

104. Stencyl - https://stencyl.com
105. Autodesk - https://www.autodesk.com
106. Unreal Engine - https://www.unrealengine.com
107. Delta Engine - https://deltaengine.net
108. MonoGame - https://www.monogame.net
109. Appsgeyser - https://appsgeyser.com
110. Siberiancms - https://www.siberiancms.com
111. Shoutem - https://shoutem.com
112. App Machine - https://www.appmachine.com
113. Buildfire - https://buildfire.com
114. Bizness Apps - https://www.biznessapps.com
115. Mobile Roadie - https://mobileroadie.com
116. Embarcadero - https://www.embarcadero.com
117. Biznessapps - https://www.biznessapps.com
118. iBuildApp - https://ibuildapp.com
119. Good Barber - https://www.goodbarber.com
120. Fliplet - https://fliplet.com
121. Gamesalad - https://gamesalad.com
122. Bubble - https://bubble.io
123. Swiftic - https://www.swiftic.com
124. Appypie - https://www.appypie.com
125. Unity - https://unity.com
126. Ionic - https://ionicframework.com
127. React - https://reactjs.org
128. Vue - https://vuejs.org
129. React Native - https://reactnative.dev
130. Node JS - https://nodejs.org
131. Sencha - https://www.sencha.com
132. NativeScript - https://nativescript.org
133. Visual Studio - https://code.visualstudio.com
134. Typescript - https://www.typescriptlang.org
135. Visual Studio Code - https://code.visualstudio.com
136. Backbone - https://backbonejs.org
137. Electron JS - https://www.electronjs.org
138. WebStorm - https://www.jetbrains.com/webstorm
139. CodePen - https://codepen.io
140. WebStorm - https://www.jetbrains.com/webstorm
141. DotNet - https://dotnet.microsoft.com

142. Alpha Software - https://www.alphasoftware.com
143. Mendix - https://www.mendix.com
144. Visual Studio - https://visualstudio.microsoft.com
145. Google Cloud Platform - https://cloud.google.com
146. Oracle - https://www.oracle.com
147. Microsoft Azure - https://azure.microsoft.com
148. Amazon Web Services - https://aws.amazon.com
149. Apache Cordova - https://cordova.apache.org
150. Xcode - https://developer.apple.com/xcode
151. AppCode - https://www.jetbrains.com/objc
152. Code Runner - https://coderunnerapp.com
153. AppSheet - https://about.appsheet.com
154. Mobiloud - ttps://www.mobiloud.com
155. Flutter - https://flutter.dev
156. Appian - https://appian.com
157. Felgo - https://felgo.com
158. Mobincube - https://mobincube.com
159. Qt - https://www.qt.io
160. Javascript - https://www.javascript.com
161. Android Studio - https://developer.android.com/studio
162. Swift - https://www.apple.com/swift
163. Firebase - https://firebase.google.com
164. Google Pagespeed Insights - https://pagespeed.web.dev
165. Chrome DevTools - https://developer.chrome.com/docs/devtools
166. KeyCDN - https://www.keycdn.com
167. Dareboost - https://www.dareboost.com
168. WebPageTest - https://www.webpagetest.org
169. Pingdom - https://www.pingdom.com
170. Devtodev - https://www.devtodev.com
171. Loom SDK - https://www.loom.com/sdk
172. OpenFL - https://www.openfl.org
173. Haxeflixel - https://haxeflixel.com
174. Git - https://git-scm.com
175. Domain Tools - https://www.domaintools.com
176. Google Code - https://code.google.com
177. Github - https://github.com
178. Bluehost - https://www.bluehost.in
179. Hostgator - https://www.hostgator.com

180. Dream Host - https://www.dreamhost.com
181. Accuwebhosting - https://www.accuwebhosting.com
182. Windows Server - https://www.microsoft.com/en-us/windows-server
183. Ubuntu Server - https://ubuntu.com/download/server
184. Oracle Linux - https://www.oracle.com/linux
185. WP Engine - https://wpengine.com
186. Hostinger - https://www.hostinger.com
187. Digital Ocean - https://www.digitalocean.com
188. SiteGround - https://www.siteground.com
189. InMotion - https://www.inmotionhosting.com
190. ISP Config - https://www.ispconfig.org
191. Vesta - https://vestacp.com
192. Froxlor - https://froxlor.org
193. Xampp - https://www.apachefriends.org
194. Wamp Server - https://www.wampserver.com
195. Ajenti - https://ajenti.org
196. Apache - https://www.apache.org
197. Nginx - https://www.nginx.com
198. Lighttpd - https://www.lighttpd.net
199. Webflow - https://webflow.com
200. Framer - https://www.framer.com
201. Figma - https://www.figma.com
202. Marvel - https://marvelapp.com
203. Sketch - https://www.sketch.com
204. Axure - https://www.axure.com
205. Proto - https://proto.io
206. Adobe XD - https://www.adobe.com/products/xd.html
207. FlowMapp - https://www.flowmapp.com
208. Visual Sitemaps - https://visualsitemaps.com
209. Wireframe - https://wireframe.cc
210. Optimal Workshop - https://www.optimalworkshop.com
211. Balsamiq - https://balsamiq.com/wireframes
212. FluidUI - https://www.fluidui.com
213. NinjaMock - https://ninjamock.com
214. Cacoo - https://cacoo.com
215. Quant UX - https://quant-ux.com
216. Mockplus - https://www.mockplus.com
217. Practitest - https://www.practitest.com

218. JMeter - https://jmeter.apache.org
219. Sauce Labs - https://saucelabs.com
220. Appium - https://appium.io
221. Selenium - https://www.selenium.dev
222. Testim - https://www.testim.io
223. Gatling - https://gatling.io
224. Telerik - https://www.telerik.com
225. Microfocus - https://www.microfocus.com
226. Radview - https://www.radview.com
227. Lambdatest - https://www.lambdatest.com
228. Soap UI - https://www.soapui.org
229. Invicti - https://www.invicti.com
230. Ontestpad - https://ontestpad.com
231. Gurock - https://www.gurock.com
232. Blazemeter - https://www.blazemeter.com
233. Headspin - https://www.headspin.io
234. Abstract - https://www.abstractui.com
235. UXPin - https://www.uxpin.com
236. Maze - https://maze.co
237. Foundation - https://get.foundation
238. Bitly - https://bitly.com
239. Cuttly - https://cutt.ly
240. TinyURL - https://tinyurl.com/app
241. Bit - https://bit.do
242. Rebrandly - https://rebrandly.com
243. Shortest - https://shorte.st
244. T2mio - https://t2mio.com
245. Replug - https://replug.io
246. Retargetkit - https://retargetkit.com
247. Shrtfly - https://shrtfly.com
248. UX9 - https://ux9.de
249. Shorturl - https://shorturl.is
250. Rocketlink - https://rocketlink.io
251. Joturl - https://joturl.com
252. Sniply - https://sniply.io
253. Capsulink - https://www.capsulink.com
254. Pixelme - https://www.pixelme.me
255. LinklyHQ - https://linklyhq.com

256. Scribus - https://www.scribus.net
257. Webpack - https://webpack.js.org
258. Polymer App - https://polymer-app.com
259. Docker - https://www.docker.com
260. Kubernetes - https://kubernetes.io
261. Codeigniter - https://codeigniter.com
262. Laravel - https://laravel.com
263. Django - https://www.djangoproject.com

CHAPTER XVIII

Social Media + Community

Meetings and Events Management Platform, Hashtags, Influencer Marketing, Contact Verifiers, Investigation Tools, Marketing Analytics, Event Sites, Community Meetup Apps, etc.

1. LinkedIn - https://www.linkedin.com
2. Instagram - https://www.instagram.com
3. Facebook - https://www.facebook.com
4. Whatsapp - whatsapp.com
5. Telegram - https://telegram.org
6. Twitter - https://twitter.com
7. Snapchat - https://www.snapchat.com
8. Pinterest - https://www.pinterest.com
9. Meetup - https://www.meetup.com
10. Tinder - https://tinder.com
11. YouTube - https://www.youtube.com
12. Pushstart - https://pushstart.in
13. Vimeo - https://vimeo.com
14. Flickr - https://www.flickr.com
15. Agorapulse - https://www.agorapulse.com
16. Buffer - https://buffer.com
17. Zoho Social - https://www.zoho.com/social/social-media-monitoring-software.html
18. Tailwind - https://www.tailwindapp.com
19. Social Flow - https://www.socialflow.com
20. Social Pilot - https://www.socialpilot.co
21. Fanbooster - https://fanbooster.com
22. Sproutsocial - https://sproutsocial.com
23. Revive Social - https://revive.social
24. Sked Social - https://skedsocial.com
25. Sendible - https://www.sendible.com
26. HopperHQ - https://www.hopperhq.com
27. Post Planner - https://www.postplanner.com
28. Meetedgar - https://meetedgar.com

29. Brandwatch - https://www.brandwatch.com
30. Coosto - https://www.coosto.com
31. Hootsuite - https://www.hootsuite.com
32. CrowdFire - https://www.crowdfireapp.com
33. iSearch Social - https://isearchsocial.com
34. Keyhole - https://keyhole.co
35. Meltwater - https://www.meltwater.com
36. Mention - https://mention.com
37. Mentionlytics - https://www.mentionlytics.com
38. Netvibes - https://www.netvibes.com
39. Newschip - https://www.newswhip.com
40. Nexusplore - https://www.nexusxplore.com
41. Reputology - https://www.reputology.com
42. Reviewinc - https://reviewinc.com
43. Samdesk - https://www.samdesk.io
44. Youscan - https://youscan.io
45. X1 - https://www.x1.com
46. Webz - https://webz.io
47. Talkwalker   https://www.talkwalker.com
48. Synthesio - https://www.synthesio.com
49. Storyful - https://storyful.com
50. Social Searcher - https://www.social-searcher.com
51. Samdesk - https://www.samdesk.io
52. Sentione - https://sentione.com
53. Emplifi - https://emplifi.io
54. Social Links - https://sociallinks.io
55. Brand Monitoring - https://brand24.com
56. TapInfluence - https://www.tapinfluence.com
57. Rival IQ - https://www.rivaliq.com
58. Eclincher - https://eclincher.com
59. Hashtags - https://www.hashtags.org
60. Hashtagsforlikes - https://www.hashtagsforlikes.co
61. Hashtagify Me - https://hashtagify.me
62. HashtagHub - https://hashtaghub.herokuapp.com
63. Trellix - https://www.trellix.com
64. Hashtag Directory - https://www.thehashtagdirectory.com
65. All Hashtag - https://www.all-hashtag.com
66. Tweet Binder - https://www.tweetbinder.com

67. Tags Finder - https://www.tagsfinder.com
68. Tagdef - https://tagdef.com
69. Socialert - https://socialert.net
70. Social Bearing - https://socialbearing.com
71. RiteTag - https://ritetag.com
72. One Million Tweet Map - https://onemilliontweetmap.com
73. Metahashtags - https://metahashtags.com
74. Leetags - https://www.leetags.com
75. Keyword Tool - https://keywordtool.io
76. Hashatit - https://www.hashatit.com
77. Hashtracking - https://www.hashtracking.com
78. Digimind - https://www.digimind.com
79. Brandmentions - https://brandmentions.com
80. Kicksta - https://kicksta.co
81. Inflact - https://inflact.com
82. Tweetdeck - https://tweetdeck.twitter.com
83. Talkwalker - https://www.talkwalker.com
84. Buzzsumo - https://buzzsumo.com
85. Sistrix - https://www.sistrix.com
86. Bigbangram - https://bigbangram.com
87. Tagboard - https://tagboard.com
88. Hype Auditor - https://hypeauditor.com
89. Heepsy - https://www.heepsy.com
90. Hootsuite - https://apps.hootsuite.com
91. Aspire - https://aspire.io
92. Upfluence - https://www.upfluence.com
93. Emplifi - https://emplifi.io
94. Ninja Outreach - https://ninjaoutreach.com
95. Klear - https://klear.com
96. Keywordtool - https://keywordtool.io
97. Post Forrent - https://www.postforrent.com
98. Public Fast - https://www.publicfast.com
99. Scoutzen - https://www.scoutzen.com
100. Amazing Hiring - https://amazinghiring.com
101. Clearbit - https://clearbit.com
102. Discovery - https://discover.ly
103. Contactout - https://contactout.com
104. Voilanorbert - https://www.voilanorbert.com

105. Contact Plus - https://www.contactsplus.com
106. Datany - https://www.datanyze.com
107. Swordfish - https://swordfish.ai
108. Sellhack - https://sellhack.com
109. Signalhire - https://www.signalhire.com
110. Snov - https://snov.io
111. Rocketreach - https://rocketreach.co
112. Precontacttool - https://www.precontacttool.com
113. Nymeria - https://www.nymeria.io
114. Loxo - https://loxo.co
115. Improver - https://improver.io
116. Hireez - https://hireez.com
117. Findthatlead - https://findthatlead.com
118. Z Lookup - https://www.zlookup.com
119. Phone Books - https://www.phonebooks.com
120. CallerID Test - https://calleridtest.com
121. Clearout - https://clearout.io
122. Verifalia - https://verifalia.com
123. IMEI24 - https://imei24.com
124. Country Code - https://countrycode.org
125. Data247 - https://www.data247.com
126. DNSlytics - https://dnslytics.com
127. Clearout - https://clearout.io
128. Email Validator - https://www.email-validator.net
129. B2B sprouts - https://b2bsprouts.com
130. Email Hippo - https://tools.emailhippo.com
131. Xverify - https://www.xverify.com
132. Email Checker - https://email-checker.net
133. Verify Email - https://verify-email.org
134. Zero Bounce - https://www.zerobounce.net
135. Email List Verify - https://www.emaillistverify.com
136. Aeroleads - https://aeroleads.com
137. Truecaller - https://www.truecaller.com
138. Lusha - https://www.lusha.com
139. Apollo - https://www.apollo.io
140. Sales Navigator - https://business.linkedin.com/sales-solutions/sales-navigator
141. HeySummit - https://www.heysummit.com

142. Crowdcast - https://www.crowdcast.io
143. City Socializer - https://www.citysocializer.com
144. Hopin - https://hopin.com
145. Townscript - https://www.townscript.com
146. Facebook Events - https://www.facebook.com/events
147. LinkedIn Events - https://business.linkedin.com/marketing-solutions/linkedin-events
148. 10times - https://10times.com
149. Ticketbud - https://www.ticketbud.com
150. Zoom Events - https://events.zoom.us
151. Regpacks - https://www.regpacks.com
152. Eventbee - https://www.eventbee.com
153. Splashthat - https://splashthat.com
154. Eventbrite - https://www.eventbrite.com

CHAPTER XIX

Health Apps

Fitness and Nutrition Apps, etc.

1. Runkeeper - https://runkeeper.com
2. Runtastic - https://www.runtastic.com
3. Strava - https://www.strava.com
4. FitOn - https://fitonapp.com
5. HealthifyMe - https://www.healthifyme.com
6. Sworkit - https://sworkit.com
7. Suunto - https://www.suunto.com
8. Mapmyfitness - https://www.mapmyfitness.com
9. Connect Garmin - https://connect.garmin.com
10. Fitocracy - https://www.fitocracy.com
11. Daily Burn - https://dailyburn.com
12. Charity Miles - https://charitymiles.org
13. Body Building - https://www.bodybuilding.com
14. Livestrong - https://www.livestrong.com
15. Platejoy - https://www.platejoy.com
16. MyFitnessPal - https://www.myfitnesspal.com
17. MyNetDiary - https://www.mynetdiary.com
18. Lifesum - https://lifesum.com
19. Fitbit - https://www.fitbit.com
20. Google Fit - https://www.google.com/intl/en_us/fit
21. Samsung Health - https://www.samsung.com/us/apps/samsung-health
22. Huawei Health - https://consumer.huawei.com/en/mobileservices/health
23. Apple Fitness - https://www.apple.com/apple-fitness-plus
24. Goqii - https://goqii.com
25. Racefully - https://www.raceful.ly
26. Gymphy - https://gymphy.com
27. Getsweatgo - https://www.getsweatgo.com
28. Fitlab Club - https://www.fitlabclub.com
29. Kinective - https://kinective.com
30. Fitness Blender - https://www.fitnessblender.com

31. Fooducate - https://www.fooducate.com
32. Carb Manager - https://www.carbmanager.com
33. My Macros Plus - https://getmymacros.com
34. Youate - https://youate.com
35. Spokin - https://www.spokin.com
36. Ovia Health - https://www.oviahealth.com
37. Nike - https://www.nike.com
38. Relive - https://www.relive.cc
39. Open Source Fitness - https://www.opensourcefitness.org

CHAPTER XX

Entertainment + Convertors + Updates + Forums

TV, News, Radio, Podcast Platforms, OTT Apps, Weather Updates, Timezones, Currency, Unit Convertors, Calculators, Q&A Forums, etc.

1. Disney+Hotstar - https://www.hotstar.com
2. Netflix - https://www.netflix.com
3. Amazon Prime - https://www.primevideo.com
4. AppleTV - https://www.apple.com/tv
5. SonyLIV - https://www.sonyliv.com
6. Zee5 - https://www.zee5.com
7. Voot - https://www.voot.com
8. JioTV - https://www.jiotv.com
9. MXPlayer - https://www.mxplayer.in
10. ALTBalaji - https://www.altbalaji.com
11. EROS Now - https://erosnow.com
12. Viu - https://www.viu.com
13. Shemaroo - https://www.shemarooent.com
14. Discovery Plus - https://www.discoveryplus.com
15. Airtel Xtream - https://www.airtelxstream.in
16. TataPlay - https://www.tataplay.com
17. YouTube - https://youtube.com
18. BigFlix - https://www.bigflix.com
19. Vi Movies and TV - https://www.myvi.in/music-videos-and-more/vi-movies-tv
20. Unscreen - https://www.uscreen.tv
21. Setplex - https://setplex.com
22. Dacast - https://www.dacast.com
23. Muvi - https://www.muvi.com
24. IBM Watson Media - https://www.ibm.com/watson/media
25. Wowza - https://www.wowza.com
26. CONTUS VPlayed - https://www.vplayed.com
27. Kaltura - https://corp.kaltura.com
28. JW Player - https://www.jwplayer.com
29. Vimeo OTT - https://vimeo.com/ott

30. Brid TV - https://site.brid.tv
31. Apple Podcasts - https://www.apple.com/in/apple-podcasts
32. Apple Music - https://music.apple.com
33. Google Podcasts - https://podcasts.google.com
34. Amazon Music - https://music.amazon.com
35. Gaana - https://gaana.com
36. JioSaavn - https://www.jiosaavn.com
37. iHeart - https://www.iheart.com
38. Online Radio FM - https://onlineradiofm.in
39. Radio India Live - https://www.radioindialive.com
40. Radio India - https://www.radioindia.in
41. AccuRadio - https://www.accuradio.com
42. Streamfinder - https://streamfinder.com
43. Streema - https://streema.com
44. Tunein - https://tunein.com
45. Radio Net - https://www.radio.net
46. Podcasts - https://www.podcasts.com
47. Podchaser - https://www.podchaser.com
48. Podradio - https://podradio.live
49. SoundCloud - https://soundcloud.com
50. Spreaker - https://www.spreaker.com
51. Spotify - https://www.spotify.com
52. Stabl - https://wearestabl.com
53. Stitcher - https://www.stitcher.com
54. Getstream Winds - https://getstream.io/winds
55. Podbay - https://podbay.fm
56. Podbean - https://www.podbean.com
57. Vocamatic - https://vocalmatic.com
58. Podcast Hawk - https://podcasthawk.com
59. Podcast Republic - https://podcastrepublic.net
60. Player - https://player.fm
61. Overcast - https://overcast.fm
62. Pocketcasts - https://pocketcasts.com
63. Antenna Pod - https://antennapod.org
64. Castbox - https://castbox.fm
65. Blubrry - https://blubrry.com
66. The Audacity to Podcast - https://theaudacitytopodcast.com
67. Fyyd - https://fyyd.de

68. Anchor - https://anchor.fm
69. Acast - https://www.acast.com
70. Podcast Addict - https://www.podcastaddict.com
71. Radio Public - https://radiopublic.com
72. Buzzsprout - https://www.buzzsprout.com
73. Transistor - https://transistor.fm
74. bCast - https://www.bcast.fm
75. Libsyn - https://libsyn.com
76. Castos - https://castos.com
77. Soundwise - https://mysoundwise.com
78. Casted - https://www.casted.us
79. Audacy - https://www.audacy.com
80. Weatherspark - https://weatherspark.com
81. Wunderground - https://www.wunderground.com
82. Near Weather - https://www.nearweather.com
83. Accuweather - https://www.accuweather.com
84. Windy - https://www.windy.com
85. Ventusky - https://www.ventusky.com
86. Weather Bug - https://www.weatherbug.com
87. Weather Widget - https://weatherwidget.io
88. World Weather Online - https://www.worldweatheronline.com
89. MSN - https://www.msn.com/en-us/money/tools/currencyconverter
90. Oanda - https://www.oanda.com
91. Calculator - https://www.calculator.net
92. Travelex - https://www.travelex.co.uk
93. Xrates - https://www.x-rates.com
94. Yahoo Finance - https://finance.yahoo.com/currency-converter
95. 24 Time Zones - https://24timezones.com/time-zones
96. Timeanddate - https://www.timeanddate.com
97. Time - https://time.is
98. Unit Convertor - https://www.unitconverters.net
99. Metric Conversions - https://www.metric-conversions.org
100. Dateful - https://dateful.com/time-zone-converter
101. Conversion Calculator - https://conversioncalculator.org
102. All in One Calculator - https://www.allinonecalculator.com
103. XE - https://www.xe.com
104. Quora - https://www.quora.com
105. Reddit - https://www.reddit.com

106. Gutefrage - https://www.gutefrage.net
107. Blurtit - https://www.blurtit.com
108. Ask - https://ask.fm
109. The Answer Bank - https://www.theanswerbank.co.uk
110. Answers - https://www.answers.com
111. IDCrawl - https://www.idcrawl.com
112. Answeree - https://www.answeree.com
113. Stack Overflow - https://stackoverflow.com
114. Blurtit - https://www.blurtit.com
115. WikiHow - https://www.wikihow.com/Main-Page
116. Experts Exchange - https://go.experts-exchange.com
117. Stack Exchange - https://stackexchange.com
118. Ask Ubuntu - https://askubuntu.com
119. Super User - https://superuser.com
120. Just Answer - https://www.justanswer.com

CHAPTER XXI

Location + Navigation

GIS, Maps, Navigation, Travel Apps, Location Apps, Coordinate Finders, etc.

1. Google Maps - https://maps.google.com
2. Apple Maps - https://www.apple.com/maps
3. Bing Maps - https://www.bing.com/maps
4. Yandex Maps - https://yandex.ru/maps
5. MapQuest - https://www.mapquest.com
6. HERE WeGo - https://wego.here.com
7. Maps - https://maps.me
8. OpenStreetMap - https://www.openstreetmap.org
9. Waze - https://www.waze.com
10. Zoom Earth - https://zoom.earth
11. Osmand - https://www.osmand.net
12. Sygic - https://www.sygic.com
13. Arcgis - https://www.arcgis.com
14. Crime Mapping - https://www.crimemapping.com
15. Esri - https://www.esri.com
16. ZeeMaps - https://www.zeemaps.com
17. Scribble Maps - https://www.scribblemaps.com
18. Kepler - https://kepler.gl
19. Mapalist - https://mapalist.com
20. Mapbox - https://www.mapbox.com
21. Mapchart - https://www.mapchart.net
22. MapHub - https://maphub.net
23. Mapillary - https://www.mapillary.com
24. Mapotic - https://www.mapotic.com
25. 360Cities - https://www.360cities.net
26. Jumbo - https://www.withjumbo.com
27. Say Mine - https://www.saymine.com
28. Abine - https://www.abine.com
29. Open Aerial Map - https://openaerialmap.org
30. Nearmap - https://www.nearmap.com

31. Maptiler - https://www.maptiler.com
32. Latlong - https://www.latlong.net
33. Maps - https://www.maps.ie
34. ZeeMaps - https://www.zeemaps.com
35. Scribble Maps - https://www.scribblemaps.com
36. Mapotic - https://www.mapotic.com
37. Mapillary - https://www.mapillary.com
38. MapHub - https://maphub.net
39. Kepler - https://kepler.gl
40. Kartograph - https://kartograph.org
41. Hivemapper - https://hivemapper.com
42. Grass GIS - https://grass.osgeo.org
43. Maxar - https://www.maxar.com
44. Mapchart - https://www.mapchart.net
45. Mapalist - https://mapalist.com
46. Arcgis - https://storymaps.arcgis.com

CHAPTER XXII

Smart Library

Research, Articles, Books, Study Tools, etc.

1. Z Library - https://z-lib.org
2. Internet Archive - https://archive.org
3. Academia - https://www.academia.edu
4. Bioseek - https://www.bioseek.eu
5. Authorea - https://www.authorea.com
6. Base Search - https://www.base-search.net
7. ASCE Library - https://ascelibrary.org
8. Bioone - https://bioone.org
9. Bitpipe - https://www.bitpipe.com
10. Altmetric - https://www.altmetric.com
11. Academic Journals - https://academicjournals.org
12. Cambridge - https://www.cambridge.org
13. CDS Web - https://cdsweb.cern.ch
14. Core - https://core.ac.uk
15. Libgen - https://libgen.is
16. PDF Drive - https://www.pdfdrive.com
17. Gutenberg - https://www.gutenberg.org
18. Standard ebooks - https://standardebooks.org
19. ePDF - https://epdf.tips
20. Hoopla Digital - https://www.hoopladigital.com
21. Over Drive - https://www.overdrive.com
22. Librivox - https://librivox.org
23. Open Library - https://openlibrary.org
24. Open UMN - https://open.umn.edu/opentextbooks
25. Many Books - https://manybooks.net
26. Digital Book - https://www.digitalbook.io
27. Readanybook - https://www.readanybook.com
28. Smashwords - https://www.smashwords.com
29. Bookbub - https://www.bookbub.com
30. Figshare - https://figshare.com
31. Google Scholar - https://scholar.google.com

32. IEEE - https://ieeexplore.ieee.org
33. Hathitrust - https://www.hathitrust.org
34. IT Whitepapers - https://resourcelibrary.itwhitepapers.com
35. My eBook - https://www.myebook.com
36. Academic - https://academic.oup.com
37. Scribd - https://www.scribd.com
38. Yudu - https://www.yudu.com
39. Issuelab - https://www.issuelab.org
40. Science Direct - https://www.sciencedirect.com
41. Whitepaper - https://whitepaper.io
42. Worldcat - https://www.worldcat.org
43. White Papers - https://www.whitepapers.online
44. Open MD - https://openmd.com
45. Medworm - https://medworm.com
46. FileZebra - https://findzebra.com
47. Google MT - https://www.googlemt.com
48. 100 Million Books - https://www.100millionbooks.org
49. Librarything - https://www.librarything.com
50. Google Books - https://books.google.com
51. Amazon Kindle - https://www.amazon.com/Kindle-eBooks
52. Bookbub - https://www.bookbub.com
53. Flipkart Books - https://www.flipkart.com/books-store
54. Apple Books - https://www.apple.com/apple-books
55. Notion Press - https://notionpress.com

CHAPTER XXIII

Network + Connectivity Apps

IoT, Home Automation, Internet Tools, etc.

1. Virtual Box - https://www.virtualbox.org
2. Proxmox - https://www.proxmox.com
3. Opnsense - https://opnsense.org
4. Pi Hole - https://pi-hole.net
5. Mesh Commander - https://www.meshcommander.com
6. Angryip - https://angryip.org
7. NMap - https://nmap.org
8. Virtual Machines - https://azure.microsoft.com/en-us/services/virtual-machines
9. Veertu - https://veertu.com
10. Qemu - https://www.qemu.org
11. Parallels - https://www.parallels.com
12. VMS - https://developer.microsoft.com/en-us/microsoft-edge/tools/vms
13. Linux KVM - https://www.linux-kvm.org
14. VMWare - https://www.vmware.com
15. Home Assistant - https://www.home-assistant.io
16. Open Sprinkler - https://opensprinkler.com
17. Smart Things - https://www.smartthings.com
18. Google Home - https://home.google.com
19. Apple Home - https://www.apple.com/in/ios/home
20. Amazon Alexa - https://www.amazon.com/alexa-smart-home
21. OpenHab - https://www.openhab.org
22. Calaos - https://calaos.fr
23. Homegenie - https://homegenie.it
24. Pidome - https://pidome.org
25. Openmotics - https://www.openmotics.com
26. Kaa IoT - https://www.kaaiot.com
27. Thingspeak - https://thingspeak.com
28. DeviceHive - https://www.devicehive.com
29. Thinger - https://thinger.io

30. Arduino - https://www.arduino.cc
31. Raspberrypi - https://www.raspberrypi.org
32. Zoomeye - https://www.zoomeye.org
33. Shodan - https://www.shodan.io
34. Leakix - https://leakix.net
35. GreyNoise - https://viz.greynoise.io
36. BinaryEdge - https://www.binaryedge.io
37. Trace Labs - https://www.tracelabs.org
38. Netcraft - https://www.netcraft.com
39. Down Detector - https://downdetector.com
40. IP Address - https://www.ipaddress.com
41. Is the Service Down - https://istheservicedown.com
42. URL Scan - https://urlscan.io
43. Analyzeid - https://analyzeid.com
44. Linkminer - https://linkminer.com
45. Majestic - https://majestic.com
46. Wappalyzer - https://www.wappalyzer.com
47. Bgpvicw - https://bgpview.io
48. IP Base - https://ipbase.com
49. Geo Data Tool - https://www.geodatatool.com
50. IP2 Geo location - https://ip2geolocation.com
51. IP Data - https://ipdata.co
52. IP Checking - https://www.ipchecking.com
53. IP Info - https://ipinfo.io
54. IP Void - https://www.ipvoid.com
55. MY IP - https://www.myip.com
56. Shodan - https://www.shodan.io
57. SpyOnWeb - https://spyonweb.com
58. Synapsint - https://synapsint.com
59. ViewDNS - https://viewdns.info
60. Speed Test - https://www.speedtest.net
61. Buildwith - https://builtwith.com
62. Geti2p - https://geti2p.net
63. Freenetproject - https://freenetproject.org
64. Wifi Map - https://www.wifimap.io
65. Wiman - https://www.wiman.me
66. Commotion Wireless - https://commotionwireless.net

CHAPTER XXIV

Blockchain + Cryptocurrency

1. Microsoft Blockchain - https://azure.microsoft.com/en-us/solutions/blockchain
2. AWS Blockchain - https://aws.amazon.com/managed-blockchain
3. IBM Blockchain - https://www.ibm.com/blockchain
4. Google Cloud Blockchain - https://cloud.google.com/customers/blockchain
5. Alibaba Blockchain - https://www.alibabacloud.com/product/baas
6. Truffle Suite - https://trufflesuite.com
7. Remix Project - https://remix-project.org
8. Geth - https://geth.ethereum.org
9. Mist - https://www.mist.com
10. Soliditylang - https://soliditylang.org
11. Ethereum - https://ethereum.org
12. Tron - https://tron.network
13. Stellar - https://www.stellar.org
14. Corda - https://www.corda.net
15. Tezos - https://tezos.com
16. EOS - https://eos.io
17. Quorum - https://consensys.net/quorum/qbs
18. Hyperledger - https://www.hyperledger.org
19. Sawtooth - https://sawtooth.hyperledger.org
20. Blockexplorer - https://blockexplorer.com
21. Hydrachain - https://hydrachain.org
22. Eris - https://erisindustries.com
23. Open Chain Project - https://www.openchainproject.org
24. Multichain - https://multichain.org
25. Blockchain - https://www.blockchain.com
26. Metamask - https://metamask.io
27. Crypto - https://crypto.com
28. FTX - https://ftx.com
29. Mexc - https://www.mexc.com
30. CEX - https://cex.io

31. Bybit - https://www.bybit.com
32. Bitfinex - https://www.bitfinex.com
33. Coinbase - https://www.coinbase.com
34. Kucoin - https://www.kucoin.com
35. Changelly - https://changelly.com
36. Binance - https://www.binance.com
37. Zeronet - https://zeronet.io
38. Crunchbase - https://www.crunchbase.com

CHAPTER XXV

Digital Reality

Augmented, Virtual, Mixed, etc.

1. ARVR Google - https://arvr.google.com
2. Microsoft Mixed Reality - https://www.microsoft.com/en-us/mixed-reality/windows-mixed-reality
3. Amazon ARVR - https://aws.amazon.com/sumerian
4. Augmented Reality - https://www.augmentedreality.org
5. Holokit - https://holokit.io
6. Ossovr - https://www.ossovr.com
7. Zooaszoo - https://zooaszoo.com
8. WebVR Showroom - https://showroom.littleworkshop.fr
9. Hubs - https://hubs.mozilla.com
10. Adobe Aero - https://www.adobe.com/products/aero.html
11. PTC Vuforia - https://www.ptc.com/en/products/vuforia
12. Open Space 3D - https://www.openspace3d.com
13. OSVR - https://osvr.github.io
14. Aframe - https://aframe.io
15. LOVR - https://lovr.org
16. Janusvr - https://janusvr.com
17. Play Canvas - https://playcanvas.com
18. Babylon JS - https://www.babylonjs.com
19. Argon JS - https://www.argonjs.io
20. ARToolkit - https://www.artoolkitx.org
21. OpenMask - https://openmask.io

CHAPTER XXVI

Software Websites

App Stores, Open Source Tools, etc.

1. OSINT Framework - https://osintframework.com
2. GitHub - https://github.com
3. Launchpad - https://launchpad.net
4. OSS Directory - https://opensourcesoftwaredirectory.com
5. OpenHub - https://www.openhub.net
6. Osdn - https://osdn.net
7. OSINT - https://osint.link
8. Sourceforge - https://sourceforge.net
9. Osalt - https://www.osalt.com
10. Foss Hub - https://www.fosshub.com
11. Bitbucket - https://bitbucket.org
12. Apple App Store - https://www.apple.com/app-store
13. Microsoft Store - https://apps.microsoft.com/store/apps
14. Google Play Store - https://play.google.com
15. Product Hunt - https://www.producthunt.com
16. Filehippo - https://filehippo.com
17. Softonic - https://en.softonic.com
18. Informer - https://software.informer.com
19. Techspot - https://www.techspot.com
20. Filepuma - https://www.filepuma.com
21. Filehorse - https://www.filehorse.com
22. Downloadcrew - https://www.downloadcrew.com
23. Downloadastro - https://en.downloadastro.com
24. Capterra - https://www.capterra.com
25. Betapage - https://betapage.co
26. AlternativeTo - https://alternativeto.net
27. Alternative - https://alternative.me
28. Privacy Tools - https://www.privacytools.io

CHAPTER XXVII

Programming Languages

1. Python - https://www.python.org
2. Java - https://www.java.com
3. JavaScript - https://www.javascript.com
4. DotNet - https://dotnet.microsoft.com
5. Go - https://go.dev
6. Perl - https://www.perl.org
7. Swift - https://www.swift.org
8. Scala - https://scala-lang.org
9. PHP - https://www.php.net
10. R - https://www.r-project.org
11. MySQL - https://www.mysql.com
12. Arduino - https://www.arduino.cc
13. Matlab - https://www.mathworks.com/products/matlab.html
14. Rust - https://www.rust-lang.org
15. TypeScript - https://www.typescriptlang.org
16. Kotlin - https://kotlinlang.org
17. Dart - https://dart.dev
18. Julialang - https://julialang.org
19. Fortran - https://fortran-lang.org
20. Haskell - https://www.haskell.org
21. Hack - https://hacklang.org
22. Clojure - https://clojure.org
23. Fortran - https://fortran-lang.org
24. Visual Basic - https://docs.microsoft.com/en-us/dotnet/visual-basic
25. C# - https://docs.microsoft.com/en-us/dotnet/csharp
26. PowerShell - https://docs.microsoft.com/en-us/powershell
27. Scratch - https://scratch.mit.edu
28. Ruby - https://www.ruby-lang.org

CHAPTER XXVIII

Data Intelligence

Analytics, Visualisation Tools, Dashboards, Artificial Intelligence, Machine Learning, Data Scrapers, Big Data, RPA, DevOps, Data Science, etc.

1. Tableau - https://www.tableau.com
2. Power BI - https://powerbi.microsoft.com
3. Infogram - https://infogram.com
4. Knoema - https://knoema.com
5. Lucid - https://lucid.co
6. Neo4j - https://neo4j.com
7. Office Timeline - https://www.officetimeline.com
8. Piktochart - https://piktochart.com
9. Pixcone - https://www.pixcone.com
10. Pixxa - https://www.pixxa.com
11. Plotly - https://plotly.com
12. Preceden - https://www.preceden.com
13. Snappa - https://snappa.com
14. Quadrigram - https://www.quadrigram.com
15. Statpedia - https://statpedia.com
16. Sutori - https://www.sutori.com
17. Visage - https://visage.co
18. Venngage - https://venngage.com
19. Timetoast - https://www.timetoast.com
20. Timeline Maker - https://www.timelinemaker.com
21. Time Graphics - https://time.graphics
22. Preceden - https://www.preceden.com
23. Highcharts - https://www.highcharts.com
24. Zingchart - https://www.zingchart.com
25. yWorks - https://www.yworks.com
26. Visual - https://visual.ly
27. Cacoo - https://cacoo.com
28. Chartblocks - https://www.chartblocks.io
29. Chart JS - https://www.chartjs.org

30. Creately - https://creately.com
31. Databasic - https://databasic.io
32. Datavizcatalogue - https://datavizcatalogue.com
33. Data Wrapper - https://www.datawrapper.de
34. Easel - https://www.easel.ly
35. Fusion Charts - https://www.fusioncharts.com
36. Google Charts - https://developers.google.com/chart
37. Apache Graphx - https://spark.apache.org/graphx
38. Lampyre - https://lampyre.io
39. Osirt - https://osirtbrowser.com
40. Shadow Dragon - https://shadowdragon.io
41. Timeline - https://timeline.app
42. Analytics Portfolio - https://analyticsportfolio.com
43. Forensic Notes - https://www.forensicnotes.com
44. Hunch - https://www.hunch.ly
45. Pagefreezer - https://www.pagefreezer.com
46. Paliscope - https://www.paliscope.com
47. Clicdata - https://www.clicdata.com
48. Cyfe - https://www.cyfe.com
49. Dashthis - https://dashthis.com
50. Vortimo - https://www.vortimo.com
51. Databox - https://databox.com
52. Datadeck - https://www.datadeck.com
53. Datapine - https://www.datapine.com
54. Geckoboard - https://www.geckoboard.com
55. Target Dashboard - https://www.targetdashboard.com
56. Spider Strategies - https://www.spiderstrategies.com
57. Smartsheet - https://www.smartsheet.com
58. Klipfolio - https://www.klipfolio.com
59. Inetsoft - https://www.inetsoft.com
60. Truoi - https://www.truoi.com
61. Tibco - https://www.tibco.com
62. IBM Business Analytics - https://www.ibm.com/analytics/business-analytics
63. Import - https://www.import.io
64. Knime - https://www.knime.com/knime-analytics-platform
65. Looker - https://www.looker.com
66. Matomo - https://matomo.org

67. Microstrategy - https://www.microstrategy.com
68. Mljar - https://mljar.com
69. Oracle BA - https://www.oracle.com/business-analytics/analytics-platform
70. Orange Data Mining - https://orangedatamining.com
71. Datarobot - https://www.datarobot.com
72. Pyramid Analytics - https://www.pyramidanalytics.com
73. Qlik - https://www.qlik.com
74. Rapid Miner - https://rapidminer.com
75. Sisense - https://www.sisense.com
76. Talend - https://www.talend.com
77. Board - https://www.board.com
78. Google Cloud ML - https://cloud.google.com/automl
79. AWS ML - https://aws.amazon.com/machine-learning
80. Count - https://count.ly
81. ObservablcHQ - https://observablehq.com
82. Dataiku - https://www.dataiku.com
83. Displayr - https://www.displayr.com
84. Domo - https://www.domo.com
85. Data Studio - https://marketingplatform.google.com/about/data-studio
86. H2O AI - https://h2o.ai
87. Hitachi Vantara - https://www.hitachivantara.com/en-us/home.html
88. Alteryx - https://www.alteryx.com
89. BigML - https://bigml.com
90. WebHarvy - https://www.webharvy.com
91. Web Robots - https://webrobots.io
92. Web Scraper - https://webscraper.io
93. Zyte - https://www.zyte.com
94. Scrapestorm - https://www.scrapestorm.com
95. Scrapestak - https://scrapestack.com
96. Proweb Scraper - https://prowebscraper.com
97. Parsehub - https://www.parsehub.com
98. Mozenda - https://www.mozenda.com
99. Listly - https://www.listly.io
100. 80legs - https://80legs.com
101. Import - https://www.import.io
102. Diffbot - https://www.diffbot.com
103. Data Miner - https://dataminer.io

104. Crawly - https://crawly.diffbot.com
105. Common Crawl - https://commoncrawl.org
106. Agenty - https://agenty.com
107. Siren - https://siren.io
108. Pagescreen - https://pagescreen.io
109. Sken - https://www.sken.io
110. Visual Ping - https://visualping.io
111. Python - https://www.python.org
112. Android Studio - https://developer.android.com/studio
113. Portainer - https://www.portainer.io
114. Anaconda - https://www.anaconda.com
115. TensorFlow - https://www.tensorflow.org
116. Keras - https://keras.io
117. OpenCV - https://opencv.org
118. Pandas - https://pandas.pydata.org
119. Numpy - https://numpy.org
120. Solr Apache - https://solr.apache.org
121. Cassandra - https://cassandra.apache.org
122. GridGain - https://www.gridgain.com
123. Mathworks - https://www.mathworks.com
124. Labview - https://www.ni.com/en-in/shop/labview.html
125. Apache Hadoop - https://hadoop.apache.org
126. Intelligent Apps - https://www.microsoft.com/en-us/AI/intelligent-apps
127. UI Path - https://www.uipath.com
128. Automation Anywhere - https://www.automationanywhere.com
129. Raygun - https://raygun.com
130. Ansible - https://www.ansible.com
131. Puppet - https://puppet.com
132. Kubernetes - https://kubernetes.io
133. Docker - https://www.docker.com
134. Jenkins - https://www.jenkins.io
135. Git - https://git-scm.com
136. Bamboo - https://www.atlassian.com/software/bamboo
137. Gradle - https://gradle.org
138. Kaggle - https://www.kaggle.com/datasets
139. Prometheus - https://prometheus.io
140. MarkMonitor - https://www.markmonitor.com

141. Maltego - https://www.maltego.com
142. CMake - https://cmake.org
143. Terraform - https://www.terraform.io
144. Bower - https://bower.io
145. Apache Maven - https://maven.apache.org
146. Nagios - https://www.nagios.org
147. Talend - https://www.talend.com
148. GoSpotCheck - https://www.gospotcheck.com
149. Mozenda - https://www.mozenda.com
150. Octoparse - https://www.octoparse.com
151. Onbase - https://www.hyland.com/en/onbase
152. Amazon Redshift - https://aws.amazon.com/redshift
153. BigQuery - https://cloud.google.com/bigquery
154. Snowflake - https://www.snowflake.com
155. Alteryx - https://www.alteryx.com
156. Domino Datalab - https://www.dominodatalab.com
157. Rapid Miner - https://rapidminer.com
158. SAS - https://www.sas.com
159. Spark - https://spark.apache.org
160. D3JS - https://d3js.org
161. Jupyter - https://jupyter.org
162. Matplotlib - https://matplotlib.org
163. NLTK - https://www.nltk.org
164. Scikit Learn - https://scikit-learn.org
165. Weka - https://www.weka.io
166. Pandas - https://pandas.pydata.org
167. Scrapy - https://scrapy.org
168. Knime - https://www.knime.com
169. Apache Hadoop - https://hadoop.apache.org
170. IBM DC - https://www.ibm.com/products/data-capture-and-imaging

CHAPTER XXIX

Career + Work

Career Sites, Freelancing Portals, AI powered Resume and Profile Builders, etc.

1. LinkedIn - https://www.linkedin.com
2. Naukri - https://www.naukri.com
3. Indeed - https://www.indeed.com
4. Glassdoor - https://www.glassdoor.co.in
5. TimesJobs - https://www.timesjobs.com
6. Monster - https://www.monsterindia.com
7. Angel - https://angel.co
8. Ladders - https://www.theladders.com
9. Linkup - https://www.linkup.com
10. Google Jobs - https://jobs.google.com
11. Ziprecruiter - https://www.ziprecruiter.com
12. Parchment - https://www.parchment.com
13. Mighty Recruiter - https://www.mightyrecruiter.com
14. Careerbuilder - https://www.careerbuilder.com
15. Bayt - https://www.bayt.com
16. Campus Career Center - https://campuscareercenter.com
17. Dice - https://www.dice.com
18. Eurojobs - https://eurojobs.com
19. SimplyHired - https://www.simplyhired.com
20. Seek - https://www.seek.com.au
21. Reed - https://www.reed.co.uk
22. Shine - https://www.shine.com
23. IIM Jobs - https://www.iimjobs.com
24. Freshersworld - https://www.freshersworld.com
25. Snagajob - https://www.snagajob.com
26. Jobgrin - https://jobgrin.co.in
27. Getwork - https://getwork.com
28. Craigslist - https://craigslist.org
29. Wisdom Jobs - https://www.wisdomjobs.com
30. Jobsite - https://www.jobsite.co.uk

31. Careerjet - https://www.careerjet.co.in
32. Upwork - https://www.upwork.com
33. Guru - https://www.guru.com
34. Fiverr - https://www.fiverr.com
35. Freelancer - https://www.freelancer.com
36. Outsourcely - https://www.outsourcely.com
37. People Per Hour - https://www.peopleperhour.com
38. Free Up - https://freeup.net
39. Workhoppers - https://www.workhoppers.com
40. Hubstaff - https://talent.hubstaff.com
41. Flexjobs - https://www.flexjobs.com
42. Scouted - https://scouted.io
43. Xing - https://www.xing.com
44. Cvviz - https://cvviz.com
45. Hiration Resume Builder - https://www.hiration.com
46. Resume Builder - https://www.resumebuilder.org
47. Zety - https://zety.com
48. Resume - https://resume.io
49. Resume Coach - https://www.resumecoach.com
50. Jobscan - https://www.jobscan.co
51. Resumonk - https://www.resumonk.com
52. My Perfect Resume - https://www.myperfectresume.com
53. Canva Resume Builder - https://www.canva.com/create/resumes
54. Visual CV - https://www.visualcv.com
55. Resume - https://www.resume.com
56. Novo Resume - https://novoresume.com
57. CV Maker - https://www.cvmaker.com
58. Enhance CV - https://enhancv.com
59. Cake Resume - https://www.cakeresume.com
60. Resumup - https://resumup.com
61. Kickresume - https://www.kickresume.com
62. Rezi - https://www.rezi.ai
63. Wozber - https://www.wozber.com
64. Cultivated Culture - https://cultivatedculture.com
65. Live Career - https://www.livecareer.com
66. Skill Roads - https://skillroads.com
67. Resumaker - https://resumaker.ai
68. Resumegenius - https://resumegenius.com

69. Resumestar - https://www.resumestar.io
70. CV Jury - https://cvjury.com

eCommerce Marketplaces

1. Amazon - https://www.amazon.com
2. Flipkart - https://www.flipkart.com
3. Snapdeal - https://www.snapdeal.com
4. Walmart - https://www.walmart.com
5. Aliexpress - https://www.aliexpress.com
6. eBay - https://www.ebay.com
7. Alibaba - https://www.alibaba.com
8. eBid - https://www.ebid.net
9. Etsy - https://www.etsy.com
10. Depop - https://www.depop.com
11. Quikr - https://www.quikr.com
12. Overstock - https://www.overstock.com
13. Redbubble - https://www.redbubble.com
14. Shopee - https://shopee.com
15. Mercadolibre - https://www.mercadolibre.com
16. Google Shopping - https://shopping.google.com
17. Target - https://www.target.com
18. Otto - https://www.otto.de
19. Rakuten - https://www.rakuten.com
20. Costco - https://www.costco.com
21. OSO Commerce - https://www.oscommerce.com

Epilogue

"Let's Make IT Simple" is my genuine effort that aims to benefit the world community. This idea of creating a smart resource library was truly a tough challenge. Believe me, I had to research, validate and crosscheck almost every word and line in this book. My journey during this whole process was filled with experiments, tests, experiences and best relevant choices.

Resources listed in this book are numbered serially, just for the sake of easy navigation. Their serial numbers do not compare, rank or sort those resources in any manner.

Technology is constantly upgrading and so, its scope too is ever expanding. I've tried my best to cover all major resources applicable in various domains. Still, I know that there is an ocean of unexplored resources lying out there somewhere on the web, so any suggestions, recommendations, feedbacks and additions are heartily welcomed.

While writing this one, I had primarily referred to the Free Software Foundation and Open Source Initiative websites. Wikipedia, technology magazines, websites, journals, papers, blogs, podcasts, documentaries, biopics, forums, newspaper articles, events, conferences, conclaves, surveys, polls and speeches were a part of my research.

This book is a treasure of **2500+ smart resources**, and I consider myself fortunate enough that I got a chance to find out, try, check, learn and share more about them.

I hope we possess this **power together**, and use it for the **greater good** of mankind ahead.

Let's Make IT Simple!

Thank You